The Wisdom Of Patañjali's Yoga Sutras

Published by Morning Light Press 2009

Printed on acid-free, recycled paper in Canada.

Cover Image: Dancing Shiva relief, Shiva temple, Gangaikondacholapuram, Tamil Nadu, India. 11th Century. © DeA Picture Library / Art Resource, NY

ISBN: 978-1-59675-025-8

Library of Congress Cataloging-in-Publication Data
Ravindra, Ravi.
The Wisdom of Patañjali's Yoga Sutras : A New Translation and Guide / Ravi Ravindra.
p. cm.
Includes bibliographical references.
Summary: "A new translation of: the yoga sutras of Patanjali, the ancient Indian text which sets forth the practical and philosophical foundations of yoga, presented here with extensive commentary and spiritual exercises to assist in the practice and understanding of one's own spiritual search"—Provided by publisher.
ISBN 978-1-59675-025-8 (alk. paper)
1. Patañjali. Yogasutra. 2. Yoga. 3. Spiritual life. I. Patañjali. Yogasutra. English & Sanskrit. II. Title.
B132.Y6P278612 2009
181'.452--dc22

2008037027

MORNING LIGHT PRESS

Morning Light Press
10881 North Boyer Road
Sandpoint, ID 83864
morninglightpress.com

THE WISDOM OF PATAÑJALI'S YOGA SUTRAS

A New Translation and Guide

Ravi Ravindra

Dedicated to
Madame Jeanne de Salzmann
with love and gratitude.

Without the relationship with higher energy, life has no meaning. The higher energy is the permanent Self, but you have no connection with that. For that connection, a fine substance needs to be generated. Otherwise, the energy of the body is too low to make contact with the very high energy which comes from above. Slowly, the desire of the mind for that relationship will become an organic need. You cannot force it. Higher energy cannot be forced. If you try to force it, it can lead to bad results. Gradually, you get more and more interested in it, and appalled by the lack when you are not in relationship. It may be too early to use the word, but that is love. You come to a state in which you realize that you cannot live without that relationship. Nothing has significance or meaning without it.

—Madame de Salzmann

Table of Contents

INTRODUCTION

Om
tat savitur varenyam
bhargo devasya dhimahi
dhiyo yo nah prachodayat.
Rig Veda (iii, 62, 10)

Let us bring our mind
to dwell in the radiance of Divine Truth.
May Truth inspire our reflections.

Throughout history, there has been only one serious concern of all spiritual searchers: How can our whole being be in harmony with universal Truth? This is not only a question for the mind; it is not a question of figuring out the Truth, but it is the central question of our life: How can we become a suitable instrument for the Truth to be expressed? This Truth has been variously labeled Brahman, Allah, God, the Holy Spirit, the Absolute, Ultimate Reality, the Sacred, or simply That. There are many other names, but none of these captures the Real, for as the Tao Te Ching says, "The Tao that can be named is not the Eternal Tao."

All spiritual traditions point to a reality which cannot be expressed. Each of these traditions speaks of this reality differently—they use different languages, different approaches, different metaphors to call us to orient ourselves to this reality. Differences in expression are natural, for the traditions have arisen in different places and at different times. The language used and the metaphors which make sense will depend upon the context and upon our own background. It is useful to study different traditions in order to be free of attachment to any one way of expressing what is beyond expression. Different expressions can help us go beyond all expression.

Sages of every spiritual tradition have insisted that the subtle vibrations which constitute the level of reality we call the Real are always present and that they pervade all space. The place where each one of us is now, is filled with the Holy Spirit or the Buddha-mind. In general, we do not experience this, but if we had a properly tuned instrument, that is, if our organism were rightly aligned and truly sensitive, we would be in touch with the Absolute.

All spiritual traditions, whether of the East or of the West, recognize that God or Truth is radically different from anything we know or can know and other than anything we can project or imagine. However useful philosophical or theological discussions, or icons and idols, or dancing and chanting may be in focusing our attention and in pointing the way to the Truth, a glimpse of the Real far supersedes any idea, any image or any feeling. "There the mind recoils on itself in wonderment," says an Upanishad. In every spiritual tradition, God is Wholly Other, *Totaliter Aliter*. As Meister Eckhart said, "If there were a God of whom I had any idea, it would not be worth having him as God." Our idea of God is always a projection of our own mind and therefore limited. What we can truly say about God is that God is indescribable and unknowable. But although we cannot know God, we can be known by God and we can experience the Real.

Although the Real transcends all forms and is wholly other than anything that has been conceived or can be conceived, and it is radically different from myself as felt or known, the great mystery is that the Unknown and Unknowable God, Brahman, is also the Real I, the Atman or *Purusha*, which dwells deep within myself.

The outstanding feature of the Indic spiritual traditions is the assertion that the Wholly Other is Intimately Myself. This is resoundingly affirmed by all the sages in India, from the most ancient to the contemporary masters. The philosophical articulations may be different, the practices suggested by them may vary in emphasis, but they all speak of the fundamental Oneness of all there is. This is true of Dirghatamas, Yajñavalkya, Kapila, Patañjali, Gautama Buddha, Mahavira, Krishna, Nagarjuna, Shankara, Ramanuja, Kabir, Nanaka, Ramakrishna, Aurobindo, Krishnamurti, and all the sages in the long line of Indian rishis, and seers. Ramana Maharishi put it very succinctly, "There are no others."

All our effort in spiritual search, which is what yoga is, is to allow ourselves to become more and more transparent to the Real, which is eternal and present everywhere, both within ourselves as well as outside ourselves. In the language of Patañjali, this Real is Purusha, the Transcendent Being in each person. Purusha is the real knower and the sole knower. Anything that can be known is not Purusha. The search for God is also the search for our deepest self. It is the search to allow ourselves to be seen and known by Purusha, the only Real Seer. That vision is not only of the sacred but from the sacred.

In the *Yoga Sutras*, Patañjali emphasizes that Purusha knows not with the mind but through the mind, a realization echoed by William Blake when he said, "I see not with the eyes but through the eyes." The mind, the instrument of perception, interferes less and less as it becomes freer and freer of subjectivity. The progressive freedom to be attained in yoga is an increasing freedom not for myself but from myself. Then the mind can become a proper instrument of perception and can act in the service of the Real.

The development of this freedom requires the cultivation of a steady and impartial attention as well as a growing discernment (*viveka*) which can distinguish between Purusha and what is not Purusha. The cultivation of a steady attention, or of "total attention" in the language of J. Krishnamurti, is the first aim of yoga as taught in the *Yoga Sutras*. Levels of attention are intimately correlated with levels of consciousness and levels of being.

There are many qualities of attention from the most superficial and personal to the level in which God's attention works through us. St. Paul said, "I live but not I, Christ liveth in me." In the language of Patañjali, Purusha attends through the purified mind which itself is a part of *Prakriti*.

The *Yoga Sutras* is a brief text which has had an immense influence on the spiritual traditions in India as well as on Sufism and perhaps on early Christianity. It is the earliest known systematic statement of the philosophical insights and practical psychology that define yoga. It is dated by scholars at some time between the third century BCE and the third century CE. Patañjali, the great sage, is regarded as the compiler of these aphoristic remarks gathered from a longstanding tradition. The sutra (literally meaning "thread") literature is a genre in which teachings are expressed in abbreviated and mnemonic form which need to be made our own by wrestling with them, standing under them and being open to their profundity.

In the Hindu Divine Trinity, Brahma is the creator, Vishnu is the preserver and Shiva is the awakener. Shiva is the Lord of dance, of theater, of music and of grammar—all different ways for the transformation of our being. He is the Lord of Yoga, embodying stillness and total attention. In the images of Shiva dancing, he dances on Muhyalaka, the demon of forgetfulness. The interpretation of Shiva as the destroyer results from the role he plays as he destroys inattention, heedlessness, attachment to the transient and addiction to the identification with our small isolated self. Shiva destroys what impedes transformation into a greater life. The union of Purusha and Prakriti is the union of Shiva and Shakti, of eternity and time, of heaven and earth. Salutations to Shiva, the Awakener from Above!

In the yoga tradition, Patañjali is regarded as an incarnation of Shesha Naga, the mighty serpent, embodying strength, energy and wisdom. Philosophy is for Patañjali, as poetry is for John of the Cross, a way of expressing a vision from on high. Patañjali is not interested in argument; he says what he sees. Philosophy for him is an experiential science. Patañjali's *Yoga Sutras* is a teaching of a psychological practice based on a spiritual vision, the vision of a still mind. He is a teacher who gives practical instructions for yoga, the work required in order to be more and more related to the Real.

The teaching of Patañjali, as expressed in the *Yoga Sutras*, is transformational. To the extent we can understand it—if we can stand under the benediction of the teaching—and practice it, we can also participate in the third eye vision which Patañjali brings and a yogi aspires to. "You have eyes but you do not see," is one of the very few remarks of Christ to be found in all the gospels. Patañjali shows us who or what in us is the real seer, and assists us to look from that level.

In what follows, we will explore the *Yoga Sutras* in order to gain insight about the various levels of attention within ourselves and about about the possibility of cultivating a steady, impartial and free attention which can relate us to subtler levels of reality. Although the *Yoga Sutras* is the text to be studied, the primary purpose of this exploration is self-study so that depths within may be discovered. Great texts can inspire us, and call us. Since they come from a higher level of understanding, they cannot be understood by us as we are. What we understand is within our ken. We need to be disturbed by the great texts and scriptures which can provide practical aid for the transformation of our consciousness, of our being, of our lives. By wrestling with these texts, and not by argumentation, we gain understanding.[1]

It is hoped that the readers will have an existential engagement with this study. Some suggestions are made for a practical exploration to aid the search for self-knowledge; these are gathered in a separate section at the end of the book.

Each verse of the text is considered, not for the sake of a textual exegesis of the *Yoga Sutras*, but in order to garner the wisdom of the yoga tradition expressed in these sutras. The *Yoga Sutras* make a call and if we can respond with willingness, effort, gratitude and humility, a connection with higher levels of reality is facilitated.

The commentary is accompanied by a new translation of the *Yoga Sutras* which is intended to help illuminate this text. This translation has been influenced by a careful reading of the original Sanskrit, by the insights of the sages and by a feeling of respect for the radical teaching for transformation contained in the text. The original Sanskrit is included in the Devanagari script, along with the Latin transcription for each sutra. The appropriate diacritical marks, following the usual scholarly conventions, are used in the transliteration, but when Sanskrit terms are used throughout the commentary, the words are spelled phonetically.

There are many interpretations of this text which are reflected in different translations. The variation partly depends on the attitude which the translator or the interpreter has, especially the attitude to the relationship between the body and the spirit, or in the language of Patañjali between Prakriti and Purusha.

Sanskrit is a rich and subtle language and many of the terms cannot be translated adequately using any single English word. Since the translation cannot be exact, after a discussion of their meanings, the words for some of the central ideas are left untranslated. These words are included in the glossary at the end of the book.

My own search started a long time ago, perhaps even in some previous life. One incident from my childhood stands out in my mind. My father was a distinguished lawyer who was usually very busy. On the few occasions when he had some leisure, his great pleasure was to sit in the sun in the enclosed courtyard with a stack of poetry books in Hindi, Punjabi, Urdu, English, Persian and Sanskrit. He would sometimes spend several hours reading poems in these various languages. If one of us urchins happened to pass by, he would read aloud what he was then reading. On one such occasion, when I was about thirteen years old, he read aloud to me a passage from the Bhagavad Gita in Sanskrit and then translated it into Hindi. Now more than half a century later, I can recite the passage in Sanskrit and give the exact reference, but at that time I did not ask for the details. The remark of Krishna which he read was: "At the end of many births, a wise man comes to me, realizing that all there is is Krishna. Such a person is a great spirit and very rare" (BG 7:19).

I had no idea how to understand that all there is is Krishna but it was clear that my father had been quite moved by the passage. He turned to me and spoke almost choked with feeling, "You know, Ravi, I can tell you the words, but I don't understand the reality of it." Here was a highly educated man, much respected in the society, and to us young boys, almost a god-like figure. And he was saying that he did not understand what was being said by Krishna. He continued, "I wish for you that you will meet people in your life who will help you understand the reality of what Krishna is saying."

Since then, although certainly not always consciously, the search for a level of understanding in which the unhearable can be heard and the unseeable can be seen—not believed or accepted on faith, but experienced directly—has been a driving force. The search to understand that all there is is Krishna, that everything is permeated by, emerges from and is sustained by One Divine and Sacred energy is an unfinished project for me, but the project sustains me and gives meaning to my activities.

This search has led me to study science, philosophy, religion and scriptures, and to learn from many wise people. In my reading of the *Yoga Sutras* I have been influenced by many sacred texts, especially the Bhagavad Gita and the gospels, both canonical and non-canonical. I am indebted to many sages, especially to J. Krishnamurti[2] with whom I had many conversations over a period of twenty years, and to my teacher, Madame Jeanne de Salzmann.[3] She had asked me about yoga many times in different contexts. In a way, this book is a partial response to her as my understanding of yoga has been informed by her teaching.

1 For a brief and general introduction to yoga, please see R. Ravindra, "Yoga: The Royal Path to Freedom" in *The Spiritual Roots of Yoga*. This article originally appeared in *Hindu Spirituality: Vedas through Vedanta*. Ed. K. Sivaraman (New York: Crossroads Publishers, 1989). Vol. 6 of *World Spirituality: An Encyclopedic History of the Religious* Quest. *The Spiritual Roots of Yoga* should be considered a companion volume to the present one and several articles in that book will be referred to in this text.

2 Please see R. Ravindra, *J. Krishnamurti: Two Birds on One Tree* and *Centered Self Without Being Self-Centered: Remembering Krishnamurti.*

3 Madame Jeanne de Salzmann was given the responsibility for Gurdjieff's teaching, called the Work, by Gurdjieff before his death in 1949. She fulfilled her obligations with an extraordinary intelligence and force until her death in 1990 at the age of one hundred and one. Even though her main work was concerned with the transformation of her many pupils to a new level of understanding, she was also responsible for the publication of the books by Gurdjieff, for the production of several films of the Movements and of the film *Meetings with Remarkable Men* directed by Peter Brook, and for the establishment of the Gurdjieff Foundations in Paris, London, and New York. All the remarks attributed to her in this book, unless otherwise identified, are taken from R. Ravindra, *Heart Without Measure: Gurdjieff Work With Madame de Salzmann.*

Samadhi Pada

■

Timeless Insight

The Teaching of Yoga

Yoga Here and Now

1.1

अथ योगानुशासनम्

atha-yoga-anuśāsanam

Here, now, is the teaching of yoga.

The very opening aphorism presents a challenge. It could simply be a statement placed at the beginning of an exposition of yoga. However, it is much more instructive to see in it an invitation to practice yoga always and everywhere. Yoga does not require sitting on a cushion in meditation and it is not limited to a specified hour or a particular posture. Each moment is the right moment and the present moment is the best one. Each place is the right place—the place where I now am can be a sacred space.

As Madame de Salzmann said "It is important to work now. Now is the only possibility, not later. To realize this possibility something is required from you."

The conditions right now are the conditions we need for our work. It is not a matter of waiting until the conditions are better, when the situation is calmer or when we have more time, or more information. Now, in the midst of our daily life, engaged in our professions and households, we can and should undertake the practice of yoga. If not now, when?

The word "yoga" is derived from the root "yuj" meaning "to unite." This word is a cognate of the English word "yoke." It speaks of an integration of all aspects within a human being as well as of the connection with subtler levels of reality. Any spiritual path towards this integration may be called a yoga. Thus, yoga is both the goal and the way to the goal. When one is in yoga, one is *yukta*. The root meaning of "yoga" is very close to that of "religion" which also means joining or reuniting with the Spirit.[1]

Whenever searchers engage in impartial self-observation, they recognize that it is difficult to have the kind of steady attention which is needed for any sustained study. The cultivation of a non-fluctuating attention requires a discipline, a *sadhana* (practice). The *sadhaka*, the one who undertakes sadhana, needs to have the attitude of a disciple—a willingness to search, to listen, to change. There is a mutuality of relationship between a discipline and a disciple: there can be no disciple without a discipline, and no discipline can endure without some disciples.

Teachers teach for the sake of transformation. The great teachers did not teach in order to win disciples. The Buddha did not teach, nor did Christ, to convince anyone or to win converts. These masters taught those who saw that they could learn from these teachers, and who brought the appropriate attitude of learning. Patañjali brings a vision from a still mind, often presenting various alternative approaches impartially, without taking sides. This can be a teaching for those who can and would learn from it.

As we become aware of the fact that there are various levels of reality, and that we need to have a more sensitive body and a more receptive mind to correspond with subtler levels, we are drawn to a teaching which can assist us in the requisite transformation of our being. This is what the discipline of yoga can bring. We need to do our part in the practice, and walk this path with diligence; as the ancient commentator Vyasa said, "Yoga is known by yoga."

Why Yoga?

1.2

योगश्चित्तवृत्तिनिरोधः

yogaś-chitta-vṛtti-nirodhaḥ

Yoga is establishing the mind (*chitta*) in stillness.

The literal translation of this sutra, "Yoga is the stopping of the movements (*vrittis*) of the mind," speaks of the process of yoga in order to reach the aim of "establishing the mind in stillness." The key words in Sanskrit are *chitta* and *vritti*. "Chitta" may be translated as "mind," "consciousness," or "psyche." The term "mind-stuff" has also been used by some translators; this has the merit of conveying an ambiguity between the structure and the contents of the mind. Chitta has both the functions of thinking and feeling, functions which are sometimes separated as belonging to the mind and the heart. From this point of view, it is better to translate "chitta" as "heart-mind" or as "psyche." In the Indian tradition, the mind and the heart are not regarded as separate, for they function together at every level. At the lower level of mind, the level of *manas*, ordinary associative thought is accompanied by lower level emotions such as anxiety and resentment, whereas at the higher level, that of *buddhi*, insight and higher thought are connected with higher feelings such as compassion and wonder.

Anyone who has attempted to pay attention to anything soon realizes how easily we are distracted and how difficult it is to have a steady attention. The movements in the mind, the fluctuations, the distractions which occupy chitta are the vrittis. The mind has a natural tendency to be anywhere but here and to be concerned with any other time but now. This state of dispersion is a feature of the usual level of the mind. This is not a personal fault, but it is a fact of the human situation. Sadhana is needed for the cultivation of steady attention, and the sutra above calls attention to this.

The many possible translations help us to realize the call of Patañjali's yoga:

> *Yoga is the stopping of the fluctuations of consciousness;*
> *Yoga is the quieting of the turnings or projections of the mind;*
> *Yoga is for the stillness of the mind;*
> *Yoga is the settling of the mind into silence;*
> *Yoga is for steadiness of attention.*

When we move away from an adherence to a literal translation, it is not wrong to suggest that yoga is for developing what the Buddha referred to as "wakefulness," or what Krishnamurti called "total attention." Vyasa, one of the earliest commentators on yoga, said that yoga is for the cultivation of the silence of the mind.

Sacred literature in general consists of both *sadhana shastra*, teachings concerned with the practice, and *siddhi shastra*, teachings which describe the goal. The latter speaks about what we will find when we reach the goal, and the former talks about how to get to the goal. Similarly, there are two ways to describe the purpose of yoga: one speaks about stopping the distractions of the mind, and the second refers to the stillness of the mind which is the result of the stopping of distractions. These are related, but they are not the same. Stopping the fluctuations is the way to reach the stillness. The first mode takes a stand in the actual and speaks of the present human situation and the need to engage in a practice to become freer of this level of the mind.

Our existence at this level has been described in various traditions as being under the bondage of sin, in the mechanicality of sleep, or under the veil of illusion. A transformational practice, a yoga, is needed to realize a different quality of being, to gain freedom and to awaken. The Buddha refused to describe Nirvana, which is the goal, other than to say that it is free of *dukkha*—that is to say, free of suffering, frustration, and unhappiness.

To adapt a metaphor from René Daumal's book, *Mount Analogue*, the peak of any mountain worth climbing is of necessity invisible, but its base needs to be visible so that we might orient ourselves in the right direction. It is difficult to know what a totally silent mind is; but we can be aware of the distractions of the mind, and we can experience a relative silence which gives us a foretaste of a radically silent mind.

The way of describing the purpose of yoga which refers to the ideal situation, to the stillness of the mind, can be helpful in calling us to turn towards this. Sages speak about what they experience, but since we do not have an experience of the ideal, our understanding of their description will be from the level of our usual mind and may stand in the way of discovering what the Real actually is, if we assume that knowing the words will bring the insight we seek. In either case, the undertaking is to make our actual situation correspond more and more to what is real; and to make the Real actual in our lives.

An accomplished yogi's mind has a quality of deep silence, which can be felt. Krishnamurti embodied this stillness of the mind. On one occasion, I asked him, "What is the nature of your mind, Krishna Ji? What do you see when you look at that tree?" He was silent for a while and then said, "My mind is like a mill-pond. Any disturbance that is created in it soon dies, leaving it unruffled as before." Then, as if reading what I was about to ask, he added with the most playful smile, "And your mind, sir, is like a mill!"

The sages have said that when the mind is silent, without distractions, the original state of intelligence or of consciousness, far beyond the capacity of the thinking mind, is present. That intelligence is more aligned to direct perception than to thinking or reasoning. The reminder from Krishnamurti, and from the philosopher Wittgenstein in a different context: "Don't think; look!" calls us to a perception of the intelligence beyond thought.

We may well say that yoga is for the purpose of cultivating direct seeing, without imaginings. Yoga leads to gnosis, a knowledge which is quite different from rational knowledge. In fact, Patañjali prefers to call the Real Knower, the Seer.

In Its True Form

1.3

तदा द्रष्टुः स्वरूपेऽवस्थानम्

tadā draṣṭuḥ sva-rūpe' vasthānam

Then the Seer dwells in its essential nature.

1.4

वृत्तिसारूप्यमितरत्र

vṛtti-sārūpyam-itaratra

Otherwise the movements of the mind (*vrittis*) are regarded as the Seer.

The essential nature, or the true form of the Seer, or the Seer's own form, is Purusha, the Transcendent Being. Purusha is steady attention without distractions, Conscious Energy or Pure Awareness. When the distractions are removed, the Seer resides in its own true nature. The true Seer is Purusha who knows *through* the mind. The purpose of yoga is to refine the mind, so that it can serve as a proper instrument for Purusha. When thinking enters, the mind brings its expectations and its projections; then we cannot see reality as it is. On one occasion, I had asked Krishnamurti what he thought of something we had been looking at. He said, "Sir, K [that is how he often referred to himself] does not think at all; he just looks."

In the Indian tradition, the emphasis has always been on seeing, but it is a perception beyond the sense organs, an enlightenment beyond thought, an insight from presence. The real knower is not the mind, although the mind can be a proper instrument of knowledge. The mind needs to become free of the distractions which occupy it and prevent true seeing. The *Yoga Sutras* emphasizes the need to quiet the mind so that there can be more and more correspondence with the clear seeing of Purusha.

Only a still mind can be attentive, and only a still mind can be the dwelling place of Purusha in its own true form. There is a quality of attention and seeing which can bring about an action in ourselves which allows a radical change to take place naturally, from the inside. I once asked Krishnamurti about the nature of this attention, what he himself called "total attention." I said to him, "What I find in myself is the fluctuation of attention." He said with emphasis, "What fluctuates is not attention. Only inattention fluctuates."

We can see from this brief dialogue that for Krishnamurti, attention is the ground, like Purusha, and it does not fluctuate. My question implied that attention can be distracted and can fluctuate—clearly a misidentification of the Seer with the distracted mind.

Patañjali begins with the statement that attention is the main concern of yoga. Otherwise the Seer—which is above the mind—is misidentified with the instrument of seeing. Steady attention is the first requirement of letting the Real reveal itself to us. The Real is always revealing itself everywhere, but in our untransformed state we are not receptive to this revelation. All the sages of humanity are of one accord in saying that there is a level of reality pervading the entire space, inside us as well as outside, which is not subject to time. The sages call it by various names—such as God, Brahman, Purusha, Spirit, Allah. However, we are not, in general, in touch with this level because we are distracted by the unreal, by the personal and by the transitory.

Just as there are radio waves originating from various transmitting stations around the world which we cannot hear if we do not have a properly tuned radio receiver, similarly the vibrations of the Holy Spirit or of the Buddha Mind or of Purusha cannot be received by us if we do not have a properly tuned apparatus. Our whole psychosomatic complex is the apparatus which needs to be tuned in order to perceive the subtle vibrations of the timeless Reality. This needs a radical transformation of the whole of our being. Yoga is the way to such a transformation. With transformation, we will be able to see our situation and the world as it is at depth, not the way we imagine it to be, or wish it to be. The cultivation of steady attention is therefore the first and most important step in this transformation.

The mind is not the real knower or Seer. The real Seer is Purusha who knows not with the mind but through the mind. William Blake said that we see not *with* the eyes, but *through* the eyes and that seeing through the eyes we see transcendent visions, visions not vouchsafed to ordinary eyes. Yoga aims at the transcendence of the mind. The purpose of yoga is to free us from the misidentification of the seer with the vrittis—or of pure awareness or consciousness with the contents of consciousness—and therefore with the mind, an instrument of perception. This misidentification of the real I with the distracted mind is akin to mistaking the shadows in the cave for reality, as Plato describes in *The Republic*.

Yoga leads to freedom from myself as I usually am—which is to say freedom from fear and self-importance—by an increasing identification of "I" with Purusha. "Not I, the I that I am, know these things," says the Christian mystic Boehme, "but God knows them in me." And St. Paul, "I live, yet not I, but Christ liveth in me" (Galatians 2:20). Simone Weil, the mid-twentieth century French mystic, quoted Madame de Salzmann saying, "Identify yourself with nothing less than God."

Yoga aims at freedom from the distractions of the mind-heart so that the seer in us could actually see the way it is; otherwise, we are misidentified with the instrument of seeing which itself is unclear and which introduces distortions. When the mind is without distraction, Purusha can see clearly through the mind. The only activity of Purusha, the Spirit, is seeing, not in the sense of visualization, but in the sense of pure awareness.

Purusha can never be seen or known, for it cannot be an object of knowledge. Anything that can be known is not Purusha, but is in the realm of Prakriti. Prakriti, which literally, means "doing outward" is the world of nature at all levels, from the coarsest to the finest. The whole of the manifest world, all matter and all processes which are subject to law are within Prakriti. Thoughts, ideas, prayers, acts of service and anything which can be considered are all in the realm of Prakriti. Prakriti is the realm which is governed by the law of cause and effect, the law of karma.

Purusha cannot be personal, just as God or Spirit cannot be personal. It is completely trans-personal, and beyond expression. Purusha is no more mine than yours. It is the source of attention and consciousness in each being. Heraclites remarked a long time ago, "Although Logos is common to all, most people live as if they had a wisdom of their own" (*Diels*, Fr. 2). Purusha is Logos, which was in the beginning (John 1.1), and is without end. It cannot not be.

Movements of the Mind

1.5

वृत्तयः पञ्चतय्यः क्लिष्टाक्लिष्टाः

vṛttayaḥ pañchatayyaḥ kliṣṭa-akliṣṭāḥ

There are five types of vrittis, which may be pleasant or unpleasant.

1.6

प्रमाणविपर्ययविकल्पनिद्रास्मृतयः

pramāṇa-viparyaya-vikalpa-nidrā-smṛtayaḥ

These are true knowledge, false knowledge, imagination, sleep, and memory.

1.7

प्रत्यक्षानुमानागमाः प्रमाणानि

pratyakṣa-anumāna-āgamāḥ pramāṇāni

True knowledge is based upon perception, inference, and valid testimony.

1.8

विपर्ययो मिथ्याज्ञानमतद्रूपप्रतिष्ठम्

viparyayo mithyā-jñānam-atad-rūpa-pratiṣṭham

False knowledge is conception with no basis in reality.

1.9

शब्दज्ञानानुपाति वस्तुशून्यो विकल्पः

śabda-jñāna-anupātī vastu-śūnyo vikalpaḥ

Imagination is thought based on images conjured up by words devoid of substance.

1.10

अभावप्रत्ययालम्बना वृत्तिर्निद्रा

abhāva-pratyaya-ālambanā vṛttir-nidrā

Sleep depends upon and leads to non-being.

1.11

अनुभूतविषयासंप्रमोषः स्मृतिः

anubhūta-viṣaya-asaṃpramoṣaḥ smṛtiḥ

Memory is recollecting past experience.

This section of the *Yoga Sutras* discusses the varieties of the movements of the mind, that is, the vrittis of chitta. All of these are in the realm of thought and time. There are many things which are advantageous or useful in this realm, or are the reverse—harmful or useless. But the important point is that there is another realm, that of the Sacred which is untouched by time, thought, and by their companions: fear and self-importance. That is the one which Krishna speaks of in the Bhagavad Gita as the domain beyond Prakriti, or the realm which Christ speaks of in the gospels when he says, "My kingdom is not of this world."

Most of us are occupied with and attached to the realm of time—approving, disapproving, proving, improving, changing, doing the right thing, making sure good things happen, or seeking reward and avoiding punishment. But somewhere deep down in our hearts we occasionally hear the whispers from the other shore, a call summoning us to seek the Real.

Vrittis occupy our mind, and we take these turning thoughts to be the Real. The purpose of yoga is to free us from the misidentification of the seer with the vrittis—or of pure awareness or consciousness with the contents of consciousness—and therefore with the mind which is the instrument of perception. This misidentification of the real I with the distracted mind is a result of mistaking shadows for reality.

All the distractions of the mind are rooted in time displaced from the present now. To be present now is not a function of time sequence. It does not refer to a moment between past and future, but refers to a quality of being, that of being present. "The Sufi is he whose thought keeps pace with his foot. He is entirely present: his soul is where his body is, and his body is where his soul is, and his soul is where his foot is, and his foot is where his soul is. This is the sign of presence without absence."[2]

Time sequence itself is a product of the vrittis, and does not hold for Purusha in its true or real form, as Patañjali asserts later in the *Yoga Sutras* (4.33).

The vrittis may be pleasant or unpleasant, positive or negative, useful or detrimental; they may be true or false but they all interfere with the ability to pay attention. Patañjali identifies the five kinds of vrittis as true knowledge, false knowledge, imagination, sleep, and memory.

Chitta is addicted to thinking, and all thought is based on past experience or past knowledge or on a projection into the future, imagining what may be. The past experiences may be pleasing to the mind-heart or they may be displeasing. We endlessly replay stories of pleasant memories as well as those which caused us suffering and we play images of future successes or difficulties over and over again in our mind. We can as easily get attached to pleasant memories as to those which cause us suffering. In fact, past humiliations and slights or injuries to our self-image have a stronger hold on our memory and our imagination than the moments of happiness and dreams of success.

The suggestion is not that thought cannot lead to knowledge, even right knowledge, but when we want to contemplate reality here and now, even valid knowledge is a distraction. As an example, if I wish to attend to a person who is suffering and sitting right in front of me but in my mind

I am thinking about the Noble Truth of the Buddha which describes the cause of suffering—as solid an instance of true knowledge as any—then I am unable to give my full attention to the person, the sort of attention which could bring about a transformation of the person and of the situation.

Good or bad thinking, leading to true or false knowledge, are all vrittis (distractions, fluctuations) for Patañjali, as it is for Krishnamurti. Thinking interferes with direct perception which requires an attention without any words or images. Purusha sees but chitta thinks and emotes. Seeing is accomplished by Purusha through the instrument of chitta, and as long as chitta is not completely emptied of its movements, there cannot be clear seeing.

All mental activity disturbs the Ground Silence. The point is that the mind can become an instrument of perception, of seeing, so that we could proceed from perception rather than from conception or thought or memory or imagination. However, for chitta to be a good instrument it must be cleansed of all blemishes, all distractions.

Wishful thinking, imagining this or that, fantasizing about this gain or that success, all in the service of self-importance; or, on the contrary, fearing one or another disaster that may befall; all these are the actions on the mind of words and images devoid of substance. Driven by fear and self-importance, we hanker after this or that, making castles in the air. This is *nishkarma kama* (the web of desires without purposive action), just the opposite of *nishkama karma* (selfless action) so highly recommended by Krishna in the Bhagavad Gita.

The sutra (1.10) above makes the suggestion that sleep is associated with a tendency towards non-being, towards non-existence, the force of Thanatos. The metaphor of sleep refers to our forgetfulness and our mechanicality, a kind of death in life and it appears in many traditions. In the Sumerian myth, a story from the ancient times, Gilgamesh forgot his real aim at the time of his final test and could not stay awake. He fell asleep and let the possibility of learning the secret of immortality slip.

In the Bible, sleep is often used as a way of speaking about death, for example in Psalm 13:4; John 11:11; Ephesians 5:14, and many other instances. Christ's closest disciples could not stay awake and keep watch with Christ in the garden of Gethsemane at the time of his transfiguration. Three times he asked them to watch, but the force of sleep was too strong and each time the disciples fell asleep.

Freedom from the vritti of falling asleep is an awakening towards real life and wisdom. When the Buddha, the Enlightened One, was asked who he was, he replied, "I am one who is awake."

To dwell on memories is clearly to live in the past. However, memory, just as valid knowledge and clear thinking, can also lead to a deepening of search for something which is in a dimension other than that of time, and therefore quite other than thought, knowledge, or memory.

> *This is the use of memory:*
> *For liberation—not less of love but expanding*
> *Of love beyond desire, and so liberation*
> *From the future as well as the past.*
>
> —T. S. Eliot in "Little Gidding," *Four Quartets*

The question then arises: Am I the seer (Purusha, which is essentially seeing, attending, awareness, pure consciousness) or am I an instrument of seeing? Or both? The fundamental question to which all serious inquiry returns is "Who or what am I?" and the accompanying question, "Why am I?" Chulwoong Sunim, the highly regarded Korean Zen Master, said that "Who am I?" is the essential inquiry at the root of all Zen koans.

The struggle to know who I am, in truth and spirit is the spiritual quest. The movement in myself from the mask to the face, from the personality to the person, from the performing actor to the ruler of the inner chamber, is the spiritual journey. To live, work, and suffer on this shore in faithfulness to the whispers from the Other Shore is spiritual life. To keep the flame of spiritual yearning alive is to be radically open to the present and to refuse to settle for comforting religious dogma, philosophic certainties, and social sanctions.

Who am I? Out of fear and out of desire, I betray myself. I am who I am not. I cover my face with many masks, and even become the masks. I am too busy performing who I think I am to know who I really am. I am afraid: I may be nothing other than what I appear to be. There may be no face behind the mask, so I decorate and protect my mask preferring a known fanciful something to the unknown.

Eleven days before his death, the great poet Rabindranath Tagore wrote a short poem in his native language, Bengali, which reads in translation as:

At the beginning of my life,
With the first rays of the rising sun,
I asked, "Who am I?"

Now, at the end of my life,
With the last rays of the setting sun,
I ask, "Who am I?"

A question like "Who am I?" is not the sort of question which can have a rational or verbal answer, once and for all. This sort of question is like a Zen koan: it can reorient our attention, acting as a spur for the transformation of our being so that we can be connected with a subtler level of the mind. Such a question is more like a quest calling for a dedicated sadhana.

The Practice of Yoga

Stay in Front

1.12

अभ्यासवैराग्याभ्यां तन्निरोधः

abhyāsa-vairāgyābhyāṃ tan-nirodhaḥ

Stillness develops through practice (*abhyasa*) and non-identification (*vairagya*).

1.13

तत्र स्थितौ यत्नोऽभ्यासः

tatra sthitau yatno' bhyāsaḥ

Abhyasa is the effort of remaining present.

1.14

स तु दीर्घकालनैरन्तर्यसत्कारासेवितो दृढभूमिः

sa tu dīrgha-kāla-nairantarya-satkāra-āsevito dṛḍha-bhūmiḥ

Continuous care and attention for a long time establishes this practice.

Stillness, or freedom from distractions, develops through practice (abhyasa). Since the mind is naturally restless and addicted to dispersion, it needs to be disciplined and controlled or called to another way of being. Human beings are born *prakrita* (natural, common, unrefined); but education can lead to a *sanskrita* (well-sculpted, cultured, educated) person.

Spiritual practice requires and creates a movement contrary to the usual tendencies of the unreformed mind. We need to make efforts to be present, to let go of distractions and we need to be willing to search for a stronger and steadier attention again and again. Any worthwhile goal requires undertaking efforts, seeing what is required, and actively engaging with the process. No amount of reading about yoga or hearing the insights of a yogi will bring freedom from distractions. The Bhagavad Gita speaks of a person who has become integrated and connected as one who "sees the Self in everyone, and everyone in the Self, seeing everywhere impartially"(6:29). The real aim and meaning of any spiritual path, of any yoga, is to bring about the right order within. The need for abhyasa presupposes that there is a process and indicates the possibility of making progress in the direction of a quieter mind.

A stillness of the mind is not possible unless the vrittis, which are constantly squandering the energy of attention, are diminished. Again and again, we need to return to seeing the distractions of the mind, and trying to cultivate steady attention. We will fail repeatedly. Then we need to try again. We need to try to stay in front of whatever is taking place. The seer in me who can watch my inattention is itself connected, more or less solidly, with attention, a part of Purusha.

For someone who is established in the quiet mind, all effort and practice seem beside the point. Such a person can rightly say that there is no path, no traveler, and that no effort or yoga is required. But when we look at ourselves impartially and see that we are not sufficiently established in the quiet mind; we realize that we need a practice. We need to start from where we are. As the Bhagavad Gita (6:3) says, what is suitable for someone ascending the hill of yoga is different from what is suitable for someone at the top of the mountain.

Our efforts to gain steady attention or an independent will may be egotistic and self-centered as we begin; we may wish for salvation or enlightenment for personal glory. If that is where we are, we acknowledge the fact, but it is important not to abandon the practice because we believe it is driven by the wrong motivation. The practice of yoga itself transforms. Yoga has a magical quality: its practice gradually reveals our motivations and small-heartedness to ourselves, and it purifies and cleanses them.

Continuous care and attention in seeing ourselves more and more impartially, suffering ourselves as we are, and being compassionate to ourselves, slowly establishes in us a stillness of the mind and the heart. Abhyasa is firmly grounded when the practice of yoga is mindfully attended to for a long time without interruption.

Freedom from the Known

1.15

दृष्टानुश्रविकविषयवितृष्णस्य वशीकारसंज्ञा वैराग्यम्

dṛṣta-ānuśravika-viṣaya-vitṛṣṇasya vaśīkāra-saṃjñā vairāgyam

Vairagya is the mastery over the craving for what has been seen or heard.

1.16

तत्परं पुरुषख्यातेर्गुणवैतृष्ण्यम्

tat-paraṃ puruṣa-khyāter-guṇa-vaitṛṣṇyam

The higher vairagya arises from a vision of the Transcendent Being (Purusha) and leads to the cessation of craving for the things of the world.

Vairagya—which is non-attachment, non-identification, disinterest, indifference, dispassion, disenchantment—brings freedom from personal desire. This desire can be for material objects or for heavenly rewards about which the sages or the scriptures speak. The freedom which vairagya brings also includes the freedom from the desire for salvation or for enlightenment, as well as the desire for great knowledge or wonderful experiences.

It is important to emphasize that vairagya is not a passive state as might be assumed from its translation as "indifference." It is a state of active attention, with a search of passionate intensity for freedom from all that is known or thought. This is the sort of indifference which Meister Eckhart regarded as the highest virtue.

Vairagya is a disenchantment with the isolated small self, cut off from the wholeness of the Vastness (the literal meaning of Brahman). It is the recognition of the insignificance of this isolated self. Ultimately, vairagya is freedom from myself, the self which is constituted by all my past actions, fears, desires, ambitions. It is a dying to myself. In the complete transcendence of the selfish "me-me-me," the real I (Atman, Purusha) can be seen to be eternally present.

Madame de Salzmann said in a meeting, "Dying to the old self is necessary for a new birth." The old self is the sum of all of our fears and desires, thoughts and knowledge; it is the whole mode of relating to everything and everyone. "Dying to myself" would certainly be the death of the self we know. We are like

A bird in a cage.
Its door wide open.
With no practice in flying,
Sitting in the cage,
Composing an ode
To freedom.

Madame de Salzmann reported, "Mr. Gurdjieff said, 'Die to yourself.' That does not mean to die. It means to die to all one's habits."

The Christian theologian-philosopher Soren Kierkegaard recognized the existential meaning of vairagya in saying that, "The highest of human tasks is for a man to allow himself to be completely persuaded that he can of himself do nothing, absolutely nothing."[3] In the Buddhist thought, as elaborated in the doctrine of *anatma* (*anatta* in Pali), the isolated self is not only impotent, it is completely devoid of being and is non-existent.

Ironically, the Buddhist and Christian understanding of the nothingness of myself is the other side of the same coin of a Vedantist saying, "I Am Brahman." The right to make such a statement, which could be misunderstood as an expression of Satanic hubris, belongs only to those rare personages who have so thoroughly emptied themselves of their egotistic self that they can be filled with the Holy Spirit or the Vastness or God. Humanity is blessed in having examples of such in the individuals like Ramana Maharishi who said, "There are no others," or Jesus Christ who could say, "My Father and I are one."

There are two distinct forces which can lead us to be disillusioned with the world or to be disenchanted with ourselves. There is the force of repulsion, arising from the recognition common to all spiritual searchers, that the world is in the sway of the Prince of Darkness, as the New Testament puts it, when we see that reward and punishment, or, putting it differently, ambition and fear are the main motivating impulses in the world. Then the searcher wishes to be free of the hold of the world. "He who loves the world is verily an enemy of God" (James 4:4). The other force is that of an attraction for something subtler, higher, and truer. Mystical literature is full of the suffering of those who have had a glimpse of the Beloved but are now separated. They yearn to be related to the quality they have tasted, but are not now in touch with.

The disenchantment with the world, with the forces behind it, and with that part of myself which is attached to the world of reward and punishment, is a recognizable stage in the spiritual journey. This is a stage of lower vairagya. The higher vairagya arises from an awareness of Purusha, the One and the Only Reality. Having been touched by it, an aspirant can no longer be satisfied with any shadow, however enchanting. The entire realm of Prakriti, the domain of cause and effect, and of visible and invisible creation in which all the *gunas* (the forces and materials of nature) operate, loses its hold on the aspirant when a contact with Purusha is made.

There are many stories in the Indian culture where the Divine Attractor Krishna (one of the derivations of the name of Krishna is from *karshati*, to attract) dances with many *gopis* (cowgirls) in the ecstasy of divine love. The gopis who have once danced with Krishna pine for His touch again and again, and are no longer satisfied with their usual worldly tasks and family life.

When the yogi is willing and able to submit the visible for the power to see, to submit the entire realm of Prakriti for the sake of Purusha, Prakriti does not disappear; she ceases to be an enchantress and becomes the real bride of Purusha, its helpmate and co-worker. Then vision and action are joined in a sacred union. Ishvarakrishna says in the *Sankhyakarika*, a text which is philosophically aligned with the *Yoga Sutras*, "Prakriti without Purusha is blind; Purusha without Prakriti is lame."

A right relationship between Purusha and Prakriti, between Spirit and body, between transcendence and manifestation, is necessary for right action. We know that vision without action is a dream. On the other hand, a Japanese proverb reminds us that action without vision is a nightmare.

Patañjali places a great deal of emphasis on abhyasa and vairagya. These two practices focus on different aspects of true individuality. In abhyasa there is strengthening of the *uniqueness* of an individual—the talents, capacities, will, determination, and the like. In vairagya, on the other hand, there is a surrendering of the individual in the service of something higher and subtler, or to God. It is a movement towards Oneness. The two together constitute a practice of active and receptive attitudes simultaneously. The development of a healthy individuality, a centered self, is necessary in order to be able to be free of selfishness and to serve. Just as only the rich can practice poverty—the poor have no choice; a strong personal self is needed in order to be able to surrender it. All the energy of activity is in the ego-self. When the Real I appears, ego can find its right place: becoming a centered self which can act without being self-centered. As I usually am, in my isolated egotistic self, I am nothing. But that recognition is not a diminishment. On the contrary, it is this very realization that opens the way to a freedom from myself and allows some taste of the Vastness (Brahman). Krishnamurti wrote in his *Journal* (p. 73), "To be absolutely nothing is to be beyond measure."

Madame de Salzmann spoke about the place of the ego: "Unless there is the I, there is only the ego. So let it be. One recognizes the presence of I from the fact that I wishes to serve. Ego does not wish to serve. But until there is the I, let the ego be. It can be useful. What else are you going to do? When the I appears, the ego automatically loses energy and becomes unimportant. It can still be there but it is not in control. When real individuality is there, the ego finds its proper place."

A Progressively Settled Mind

1.17

वितर्कविचारानन्दास्मितारूपानुगमात्संप्रज्ञातः

vitarka-vicāra-ānanda-asmitā-rūpa-anugamāt-saṃprajñātaḥ

Samprajñata is the state of consciousness in which there is an awareness of the object with thought, reflection, pleasure and a sense of a separate self (*asmita*).

1.18

विरामप्रत्ययाभ्यासपूर्वः संस्कारशेषोऽन्यः

virāma-pratyaya-abhyāsa-pūrvaḥ saṃskāra-śeṣo' nyaḥ

Beyond this, when the mind is emptied with practice, there is a state in which only the trace impressions (*samskaras*) remain.

1.19

भवप्रत्ययो विदेहप्रकृतिलयानाम्

bhava-pratyayo videha-prakṛti-layānām

This is the nature of existence for beings without physical bodies and for those who are absorbed in the womb of life awaiting reincarnation.

1.20

श्रद्धावीर्यस्मृतिसमाधिप्रज्ञापूर्वक इतरेषाम्

śraddhā-vīrya-smṛti-samādhi-prajñā-pūrvaka itareṣām

For others, this state is realized through faith, will, mindfulness, tranquility, and wisdom.

1.21

तीव्रसंवेगानामासन्नः

tīvra-saṃvegānām-āsannaḥ

It is near for those who ardently desire it.

1.22

मृदुमध्याधिमात्रत्वात्ततोऽपि विशेषः

mṛdu-madhya-adhimātratvāt-tato'pi viśeṣaḥ

Even among these there are degrees—mild, moderate, and intense.

As the vrittis are diminished, the mind goes through different stages of quietening. The first stage of a settled mind, that is to say a mind in *samadhi*, is the one in which the subject and the object are quite distinct. There is a sense of a subjective self, an awareness of myself as thinking about or reflecting upon an object or taking pleasure in it. This is called *samprajñata*, a state of quiet mind, in which the knowing subject and the object are both present and distinct from each other. This state of consciousness is very close to what Gurdjieff described as "self consciousness"—a state of being present to what is seen and to myself at the same time. This state is below the highest vairagya in which there is complete freedom from myself.

Beyond this, there is further quietening in which the contents of consciousness are dropped. This state is called *asamprajñata samadhi*, a samadhi which is empty of contents. There is no thought or thinking or emoting in this state, no sense of myself as distinct from the object.

This state of consciousness exists for those who do not have a gross physical body and are absorbed in life energies in the subtle spirit world, as is the case between two incarnations. The very fact of awaiting an incarnation or wishing for it, or hankering for it, is an indication of the activity of trace impressions. We can sometimes experience a freedom from the body in meditation which is quite free of the identification with the body-mind. However, if even the slightest fear or desire enter, the attention immediately returns to an identification with the body-mind. This is a result of the trace impressions left by the activity of the mind in the past.

This state of asamprajñata samadhi itself is quite extraordinary and is attained after repeated practice. However, this state itself is considered mild by Patañjali. It may more naturally be the state of consciousness in the state of being without a coarse physical body, but for incarnate beings it is a result of practice involving trust and faith (*shraddha*), determination and will (*virya*), mindfulness, calmness and insight.

The above sutras describe different stages of progressive settling of the mind. The degree of stillness depends on the intensity of effort and ardor.

It is good to remember that freedom from the body-mind is not only for those who are disincarnate and do not have a body-mind. The whole enterprise of yoga, as of any spiritual practice, is to assist us to become *jivan mukta*—free while still alive and engaged in the maintenance of right order in the world.

Surrender to God

1.23

ईश्वरप्रणिधानाद्वा

īśvara-praṇidhānād-vā

Samadhi—timeless insight and integration—may be reached by self-surrender to God (Ishvara).

1.24

क्लेशकर्मविपाकाशयैरपरामृष्टः पुरुषविशेष ईश्वरः

kleśa-karma-vipāka-āśayair-aparāmṛṣṭaḥ puruṣa-viśeṣa īśvaraḥ

Free of the bondage of action, the laws of cause and effect, and past impressions, Ishvara is the unique being who is unaffected by suffering.

1.25

तत्र निरतिशयं सर्वज्ञबीजम्

tatra niratiśayaṃ sarva-jña-bījam

In Ishvara lies the incomparable seed of all insight and wisdom.

1.26

स एष पूर्वेषामपि गुरुः कालेनानवच्छेदात

sa eṣa pūrveṣām-api guruḥ kālena-anavachchhedāt

Unconditioned by time, Ishvara is also the teacher of earlier seers.

Ishvara can be translated as God, defined in the sutras above as the unique being unaffected by the fruits of action or by subliminal impressions. Ishvara is the incomparable seed of all insight and wisdom, the teacher of all sages and seers. According to Patañjali, devotion to Ishvara leads to freedom from distractions and to the insight of samadhi.

In the Indian tradition, Krishna is an incarnation of the Highest God, who manifests himself whenever there is a need. As was mentioned earlier, one of the roots from which the word "Krishna" is derived is *karshati*, to attract. Krishna repeatedly says in the Bhagavad Gita that he is seated in the heart of everyone. We can recognize the Attractor, deep in our hearts, in response to whose wish and need we have taken on the present incarnation. The Highest resides in our deepest. Thus our Krishna, or our God, is something akin to our *raison d'être*, the very reason for our existence in this body at this time and in this place. If we stay dedicated to that deep seated reason, the very purpose and aim of our existence, then we will not be distracted by this or that passing wish or fancy or fear.

Surrender (*pranidhana*) to Ishvara is a total dedication to our deepest self. It is a surrendering to God, which calls for the highest vairagya, the freedom from attachment to anything less than God. But because the allurement of the lesser realities—success, gain of wealth and power, approval of others, and the like—is very strong, therefore constant abhyasa is needed. Abhyasa, vairagya, and Ishvara pranidhana are intimately intertwined and Patañjali emphasizes their importance again and again in different ways.

In the Bhagavad Gita, Krishna says to Arjuna:

> *Offering all actions to Me,*
> *Mindful of your deepest self,*
> *Without expectation, without self-occupation,*
> *Struggle without agitation* (3:30).

There are many images of God in the history of humanity. Often these are associated with power or love or justice. Examples of the images of the power manifestation of God are found in the book of Job in the Bible and in the eleventh chapter of the Bhagavad Gita. Images of a loving God are to be found in the bhakti tradition of India, especially in devotion to Krishna who is said to be the "Love Incarnation" of God, as well as in the Sufi tradition. Such images can be found in many other traditions. Many people can sense a noticeable shift in the nature of God from the Old Testament to the New Testament, from a God of justice to a God of love.

Different states of consciousness project different images of God—loving or vengeful or jealous, energetic or terrifying, and different images of God affect the nature and quality of our response to God. Different images of God will have different effects on the individual and on the culture. The image or the idea of God as wrathful and jealous will have a different effect than the image or the idea of God as loving. Similarly, whether God is regarded as male or female will have a significant impact on the culture.

In many traditions love is a fundamental quality of the Ultimate

Reality or God. It is not only a quality but a basic constituent of the Ultimate Reality. The Rig Veda (X.129.4) says, "In the beginning arose love." And the New Testament affirms: "God is love, and he who abides in love abides in God, and God in him" (1 John 4:16). The search for this love, which lies at the very heart of the cosmos, is both the beginning and the end of the spiritual path, expressed as service, mercy, compassion, and ultimately as oneness with all other beings. The core of all spiritual practice is freedom from the selfish, isolated, and isolating ego so that we can see more and more clearly and be related to all there is, more and more lovingly and selflessly. In the very last canto of the *Paradisio* in the *Divine Comedy*, Dante expresses his vision of the highest heaven:

> *There my will and desire*
> *Were one with Love;*
> *The love that moves*
> *The sun and the other stars.*

Dante speaks of love at a very high level. Although we may not be able to experience love at that level, we can recognize different levels of love within our own experience. It is a general suggestion in the Indian tradition that love at all levels, even at a relatively superficial level of sexual attraction, nevertheless participates in the cosmological movement of love, as happiness at all levels shares something of the great *ananda* (joy, bliss) pervading the subtlest levels of the cosmos.

For Patañjali, Ishvara is a unique being untouched by suffering, by any compulsion for action, by any selfish desire for this or that outcome, and by any subliminal motives. It is important to remember that the whole of the Hindu tradition regards Ishvara to be seated at depth within each person. Therefore, this God is not elsewhere; our own deepest (or highest) part is Ishvara, totally free of sorrow and compulsions.

The insight and wisdom of Ishvara are unsurpassed. It is a common practice to translate this sutra (1.25) as indicating the wisdom or the omniscience of Ishvara. But the Sanskrit word, *jñana*—which is insight, wisdom, knowledge—is always accompanied by love and compassion. Ishvara is as much all loving (Omniamorossus) as all knowing

(Omniscient). Whoever is full of wisdom is naturally compassionate; in fact we recognize that someone has gained spiritual wisdom by seeing their compassionate behavior. When the Buddha reached enlightenment, his insight was expressed through compassion as well as through wisdom. Individuals and countries with power need to develop wisdom and compassion, for without these attributes, there is a danger that the power will be used to oppress and exploit others.

Ishvara is not afflicted by time. As we will see later in the *Yoga Sutras* (4.33), the general impression that events follow a time sequence is itself a mark of a relatively limited consciousness which is superseded in the highest state of consciousness, that of *Kaivalya*. As is said of the Buddha after his enlightenment, having become freed of time (*kala vimukta*), he became a seer of all time (*trikala darshi*, the seer of three times—past, present, and future). Unconditioned by time, Ishvara is present at all times and is the teacher of yoga now, long ago, and forever.

We cannot think except in the categories of the mind, including that of time. We find a similar situation in the gospels: when Christ said, "Before Abraham was, I AM," it completely bewildered those who heard him. Similarly, in the Bhagavad Gita, when Krishna said that he taught the same yoga in the beginning to the Sun God, Arjuna was puzzled. When we hear of something which is eternal, we mentally substitute the notion of *everlasting* for the *eternal*. Whatever is everlasting still remains in the dimension of time, but what is eternal is orthogonal to the dimension of time. It does not create a shadow or a projection in history; it is not opposed to time, but it is independent of time. *Everlasting* refers to a quantitative extension in time; the *eternal* is a state of being outside of time.[4]

1.27

तस्य वाचकः प्रणवः

tasya vāchakaḥ praṇavaḥ

Om is the expression of Ishvara.

1.28

तज्जपस्तदर्थभावनम्

taj-japas-tad-artha-bhāvanam

Repetition of this sacred syllable can lead to the realization of its meaning.

1.29

ततः प्रत्यक्चेतनाधिगमोऽप्यन्तरायाभावश्च

tataḥ pratyakchetanā-adhigamo' py-antarāya-abhāvaś-cha

Then there is no interference and inward-mindedness is attained.

The sacred vibration behind "Om" is said by Patañjali to be the representative or symbol of Ishvara, and its repetition gradually yields its meaning, and has an effect on our psyche. Om is composed of "a"+ "u"+"m." The first sound "a" is the first phoneme in the Sanskrit language, and is the first letter of the Devanagari alphabet in which Sanskrit is written, the second "u" is the middle and the final "m" adds a nasalization at the end. The chanting of and meditation on Om is the oldest and most widely practiced exercise in yoga. The recitation of Om should begin from the abdomen and move up through the chest and end at the top of the head with the humming sound. In the Mandukya Upanishad, the first verse and the last five verses, of the total twelve verses, are devoted to an esoteric exploration of Om, and the three phonemes of the syllable Om are identified with the three states of consciousness which will be discussed below.

As the sutra above suggests, attending to the subtler sound behind the audible sound of Om leads to inwardness and this leads to a freedom from the impediments which prevent a clarity of mind. Inwardness, with an increasing silence of the mind, will lead to a clearer realization of the meaning of Om and of Ishvara—which is our inmost purpose and *raison d'être*.

1.30

व्याधिस्त्यानसंशयप्रमादालस्याविरतिभ्रान्तिदर्शनालब्ध
भूमिकत्वानवस्थितत्वानि चित्तविक्षेपास्तेऽन्तरायाः

vyādhi-styāna-saṃśaya-pramāda-ālasya-avirati bhrānti-darśana-alabdha-bhūmikatva-anavasthitatvāni chitta vikṣepās-te'ntarāyāḥ

Sickness, apathy, doubt, carelessness, laziness, indulgence, confusion, unsteadiness, and feeling stuck are the interruptions which cause dispersion of attention.

1.31

दुःखदौर्मनस्याङ्गमेजयत्वश्वासप्रश्वासा विक्षेपसहभुवः

duḥkha-daurmanasya-aṅgam-ejayatva-śvāsa-praśvāsā vikṣepa-sahabhuvaḥ

Dissatisfaction, despair, nervousness, and irregular breathing accompany this dispersion.

1.32

तत्प्रतिषेधार्थमेकतत्त्वाभ्यासः

tat-pratiṣedha-artham-eka-tattva-abhyāsaḥ

Dispersion is prevented by the practice of focusing on one truth (*tattva*).

There are many interruptions which prevent a steadiness of attention; these can be physical or psychological. The impediments which interfere with our practice and distract the mind are disease, apathy, doubt, heedlessness, indolence, dissipation, false vision, a feeling of making no progress in yoga, and restlessness. It is a common experience of many sadhakas that they begin by making strong efforts, convinced that the practice of yoga is both good and necessary for them, but then by slow degrees they lose interest in the practice and find themselves postponing what they had decided to try. Excuses begin to multiply as to why they will make stronger efforts on another day, when they are in a better emotional state, or when they have more time.

Such situations are not only common, they are inevitable—for the simple reason that the entire driving force of lower nature, within us as well as outside, is against our spiritual evolution. There are many mythological stories in India in which Indra, the chief of the gods responsible for the maintenance of the usual order in the cosmos which requires a commitment to the status quo, *abhinivesha*, would send either disasters or temptations to the *rishis*, who were found to be making progress, in order to waylay them from their sadhana.

The temptations of the Buddha by Mara and of the Christ by Satan in the wilderness are well-known. This should give us heart: if even these great warriors of the spirit had to struggle against the inevitable, and quite lawful, impediments, why should we be spared these difficulties? Both Mara in Pali and Satan in Hebrew mean "obstruction" or "impediment." Of course, the greater the warrior, the bigger the devil they have to wrestle with. Most of us are small warriors; and the devils we have to face are also quite small—just ordinary laziness, the tendency to postpone efforts until more suitable circumstances will be found, the need to be approved, and the like.

We can see in ourselves that these impediments result in frustration, suffering, depression, nervousness, and irregular breathing. If we find ourselves with any of these symptoms, we need to take a close look at ourselves. It cannot be over emphasized that a serious practice of yoga requires a healthy body and a healthy psyche. When faced with these obstacles, a steady focusing on one truth or principle and a sustained practice for purification of the mind are recommended. Each one of us can find a great enunciation from the sages or from the scriptures which speaks to us as the tattva to focus on and to return to. Whatever profoundly speaks to us finds some echo in the depth of our heart; it therefore also speaks of us. Examples of such great enunciations are "God is love" from the Bible or "All there is is Krishna" in the Bhagavad Gita.

Tranquil Mind

1.33

मैत्रीकरुणामुदितोपेक्षाणां सुखदुःखपुण्यापुण्यविषयाणां भावनातश्चित्तप्रसादनम्

maitrī-karuṇā-muditā-upekṣānāṃ sukha-duḥkha-puṇya-apuṇya-viṣayāṇāṃ bhāvanātaś-chitta-prasādanam

A clear and tranquil mind results from cultivating friendliness towards those who are happy, compassion towards those who suffer, joy towards the virtuous, and impartiality towards wrong-doers.

This sutra deals with our relationships with our fellow human beings. To enjoy the good fortune and happiness of others and to have compassion towards those who suffer misfortunes both require and assist a freedom from self-occupation. In turn, these attitudes help in the cultivation of a peaceful and quiet mind. To celebrate those who do good deeds and to be impartial towards those who do wrong free us from small-mindedness and rigidity of attitude.

The Sanskrit word which is translated as "impartiality" in the above sutra is *upeksha*. Sometimes this word is translated as "indifference"; this conveys an emphasis which unfortunately is associated with a fair amount of spiritual practice in India where it is mistakenly suggested and believed that a mark of advanced yogis is an indifference to social concerns or the aesthetic conditions of their surroundings. No doubt there are very high and subtle states of consciousness in which a yogi is asleep or even dead to the entire world of space and time, and when he or she needs to be taken care of by well-wishers close by. But the practice of yoga is meant to lead to more and more sensitivity to all our surroundings and relationships, and to develop an increasing understanding and compassion.

Upeksha is much closer to impartiality than to indifference. When we are impartial we do not take events personally, that is, we do not just take our own interests and ideas into account. To see more and more impartially is to take more and more into account. When others engage in actions we do not approve of, we can understand that there are compulsions—perhaps derived from past lives or from their education and upbringing or from some inner conflict—which cause them to act as they do. Far from our condemnation, they need our sympathy and goodwill, especially as we ourselves understand more and more that because of the universal law of karma evil-doers will have much suffering in their lives, present or future.

These recommendations of Patañjali seem obvious, but their practice is not so easy because most of the time we are occupied with ourselves, with our happiness or our suffering, our likes and dislikes. In general, we do not see the others as autonomous persons who have hopes, wishes, fears, and a depth within. Still, there is no escape from steady and repeated practice so that we may internalize these attitudes.

1.34

प्रच्छर्दनविधारणाभ्यां वा प्राणस्य

prachchhardana-vidhāraṇābhyāṃ vā prāṇasya

Or from attention to the outward and inward flow of breath (*prana*).

Irregular breathing is an indication of some disturbance in the mind or the heart. Patañjali suggested this in an earlier sutra also (1.31). Watching our breathing provides the most accessible test of the suggestion that whatever we pay attention to changes in quality. Breathing goes on all the time, we cannot not breathe. But if we watch our breathing, its quality changes. And in its turn, a change in the quality of our breathing affects our emotional state. While we live, we breathe. The movement of breath is required for the life of each cell of the body, yet we do not decide to breathe. Where does the breath come from? Does it belong to the individual? The source of breath is a great mystery and we are filled with this mystery each time we breathe.

"The Lord God formed man of dust from the ground, and breathed into his nostrils the breath of life; and man became a living being" (Genesis 2:7).

In all ancient languages, the words for "breath," and "spirit" are intimately connected, indicating their close relationship. Respiration is the act of receiving the spirit again and again with the air. The Sanskrit term *prana* is translated as "breath," but prana is not only breath in the usual sense of that word. Ordinary breath, the most manifest symptom of life, is only the obvious aspect of prana. Like its Chinese equivalent, *chi*, prana refers to a whole spectrum of subtle energies, manifesting at the coarse material level as ordinary breath in which we take in air through the nostrils. Our whole organism, not only the nostrils, participates in receiving finer alchemical substances, impressions, and energies. The substances we can take in from the whole field of prana depend on the depth and quality of our attention. What an accomplished yogi breathes in and utilizes is not the same substances as breathed in by a novice.

Attention to our own breathing in and breathing out, without manipulating it in any way, is one of the simplest and most helpful practices in yoga for reaching a tranquil mind. The Chhandogya Upanishad (VI.8.2) says: "Just as a bird tied by a string, after flying in various directions without finding a resting place elsewhere settles down at the place where it is bound, so also the mind, my dear, after flying in various directions without finding a resting place elsewhere settles down in breath, for the mind, my dear, is bound to breath."

1.35

विषयवती वा प्रवृत्तिरुत्पन्ना मनसः स्थितिनिबन्धनी

viṣaya-vatī vā pravṛttir-utpannā manasaḥ sthiti nibandhanī

Or from steady attention to subtler levels of sensation.

1.36

विशोका वा ज्योतिष्मती

viśokā vā jyotiṣmatī

Or by experiencing inner radiance free from sorrow.

1.37

वीतरागविषयं वा चित्तम्

vīta-rāga-viṣayaṃ vā chittam

Or by turning to those things which do not incite attachment.

The whole domain of sensations is vast and subtle. According to Sri Anirvan, a twentieth century sage from Bengal, all spiritual experiences correspond to sensations in the body.[5] Sensations caused by outer objects are received through the external senses. Finer sensations in the body which are not caused by any externally perceivable objects are received by the inner senses. Attending to subtler inner sensations helps develop the inner senses. When Christ and other sages remind us that we have eyes but we do not see, and that we have ears but we do not hear, a subtler seeing and hearing than is possible with the ordinary eyes and ears is invited. Things of the flesh are seen by the eyes of the flesh, and things of the spirit by the eyes of the spirit.

It is as if we need to open another door of perception in order to have glimpses of the reality which we cannot see as we are. We have to discover and look with our third eye, for the two physical ones see only dimly. It is only this third eye which can see the hidden sun, for as Plotinus said, "to any vision must be brought an eye adapted to what is to be seen, and having some likeness to it. Never did eye see the sun unless it had first become sun like, and never can the soul have vision of the First Beauty unless itself be beautiful" (*Enneads* 1.6.9).

Yoga practice can make us more and more sensitive to subtler and subtler sensations in the body. Paying attention to and staying with finer and finer sensations within the body is one of the surest ways to steady the wandering mind. The mind has a tendency to wander, but connecting the mind to the body through sensation helps steady it and assist it in remaining present in the here and the now.

Among the practices suggested by Patañjali for clearing the mind is dwelling on a feeling of inner illumination and joy, without conflict and sorrow. If we find ourselves without such uplifting positive feelings, it is useful to begin with the recognition of the fact that I am alive. Becoming aware of the miracle and wonder of being alive, quite naturally brings a feeling of gratitude into the heart. We can remind ourselves of the many personal and universal blessings each one of us is granted—including the air we breathe, the sunshine that sustains all life, and the earth we walk on. The same beneficent forces which brought us into this life can be invoked to bring us some contact with inner illumination and happiness. Gradually, the heart opens a little and we begin to experience the real feelings which we had hoped for.

As spiritual searchers we need to become freer and freer of the attachment to our own smallness in which we get occupied with me-me-me. Pondering on large ideas or standing in front of things which remind us of a vast scale can free us from acquisitiveness and competitiveness, and from our likes and dislikes. If we sit with an increasing stillness of the body, and attune our mind to the sky or to the ocean or to the myriad stars at night, or any other indicators of vastness, the mind gradually stills and the heart is filled with quiet joy. Also, recalling our own experiences in which we acted generously or with compassion for the simple delight of it without expectation of any gain can give us more confidence in the existence of a deeper goodness from which we may deviate.

1.38

स्वप्ननिद्राज्ञानालम्बनं वा

svapna-nidrā-jñāna-ālambanaṃ vā

Or by depending upon insights obtained in the states of greater awakening called *svapna* and *nidra*.

1.39

यथाभिमतध्यानाद्वा

yathā-abhimata-dhyānād-vā

Or by meditating on the longing of the heart.

In the spiritual literature of India, four states of consciousness are mentioned. In the Mandukya Upanishad all twelve verses are devoted to a description of the various levels or states of consciousness. The different phonemes in the sacred syllable "Om" are identified with the first three states of consciousness.

In the first state of consciousness, *jagrata*, that of the ordinary waking state, a person perceives what is outside. Perception here is an out-sight. The Mandukya Upanishad refers to this state of consciousness as *vaishvanara*—the universal one. This is the most common state of ordinary humanity which lives in sleep, as the Buddha would say, or in illusion, as the Vedantist would say, even when they are awake in the usual sense of the word. When all our perceptions are occupied with the external world, when we are happy or unhappy with the events and situations of our lives, we live in the most superficial state of consciousness.

Some people are not satisfied exclusively by the external world. They are interested not only in the visible world, but also in a more subtle reality in the world and in the self. The oldest upanishad, Brihadaranyaka Upanishad, says "Whoever departs from this world without having realized his own inner world, to him life has been of no service; it remains unlived, like the unrecited Vedas or any other undone deed"(I.4.15).

The next higher state of consciousness is that of *svapna* (literally, dream) in which a person is more awake innerly, and begins to recognize the dream-like nature of the external world. It is not a state of dreaming in the usual sense of that word. A person in the state of svapna perceives what is inside and enjoys finer aspects of reality. Mandukya Upanishad refers to this state as *taijasa*—the brilliant one. Perception here is an insight.

The next higher state of wakefulness, labeled *nidra* (literally, deep sleep) in the classical literature and in the sutra (1.38) above, is not a deep sleep in the usual meaning of these words. The states of progressive wakefulness cannot be more and more unconscious; a person in a coma is not at a higher level than the Buddha. Nidra (also called *sushupta*) is a state of awareness in which a person is asleep to the world, in a state of high vairagya. This is the state of real insight (*prajña*). It is worth quoting the Mandukya Upanishad in this context, where this third state is called *prajña*—the intelligent one. In this state, a person "entertains no desires and sees no dreams; having become unified, and thus with a wholeness of perception, consisting of bliss, facing the truth, he is the lord of all, he is the knower of all; he is the inner controller; he is the womb of all—for he is the origin and the dissolution of beings" (verse 5-6).

Beyond this state of prajña is the highest state of consciousness which is simply called The Fourth (*Turiya*) because in this state the mind is awestruck. Language is wholly inadequate to describe it. The highest state, Turiya, is identified with Brahman, the Absolute, even beyond Ishvara. About this Mandukya Upanishad (verse 7) says, "Turiya, say the wise, is not subjective experience, nor objective experience, nor experience intermediate between these two, nor is it a negative condition which is neither consciousness nor unconsciousness. It is not the knowledge of the senses, nor is it relative knowledge, nor yet inferential knowledge. Beyond the senses, beyond the understanding, beyond all expression, is The Fourth. It is a pure unitary consciousness, wherein awareness of the world and of multiplicity is completely obliterated. It is ineffable peace. It is the supreme good. It is One without a second. It is the Atman (Self). Know it alone."

In the sutra (1.38) under discussion, Patañjali is not yet speaking about the state corresponding to Turiya; that is for later when the equivalent level of Kaivalya is considered. Here he is indicating that the insights obtained in the states of svapna and nidra—states higher than the ordinary waking state—can be stabilizers of the mind. The best of course are our own insights obtained in the states of svapna or nidra. But we can also rely on the realization of the sages who obtained these insights in such higher states. Reading and reflecting upon their insights can also assist quietening of our minds.

In the last sutra quoted above (1.39), Patañjali says that we can meditate on anything that our heart desires. The important thing is not what we meditate on, but more that we meditate. And then gradually to meditate more and more on what corresponds to the innermost longing of our heart. The practice of meditation—staying with one tattva, one principle or one truth, being present to what is, being receptive and open, deeply relaxed and intensely alert, like a relaxed arrow—itself gradually works its magic in stilling the mind.

A Clear Mind

Fusion but not Confusion

1.40

परमाणुपरममहत्त्वान्तोऽस्य वशीकारः

parama-aṇu-parama-mahatva-anto'sya vaśīkāraḥ

For one whose mind is clear, mastery extends from the most minute particle to the largest expanse.

1.41

क्षीणवृत्तेरभिजातस्येव मणेर्ग्रहीतृग्रहणग्राह्येषु तत्स्थतदञ्जनता समापत्तिः

kṣīṇa-vṛtter-abhijātasya-iva maṇer-grahītṛ-grahaṇa-grāhyeṣu tat-stha-tad-añjanatā samāpattiḥ

When the vrittis are diminished, the mind is like a clear diamond which reflects what is before it. Then fusion (*samapatti*) of perceiver, perceiving, and the object of perception takes place.

The purification of the mind is a cleansing of the doors of perception. The awakening of the senses is as necessary as the awakening of the mind and of the heart. It is said that the late nineteenth century sage, Ramakrishna, occasionally went into samadhi on seeing a beautiful sunrise over the river Ganga. Clear perception is not limited to a particular scale, and extends from the smallest to the largest, from elementary particles to the entire cosmos.

As the vrittis, the movements of the mind, are diminished, the mind becomes like a clear diamond reflecting the suchness of whatever is attended to, large or small. In this state of samapatti, the seeing, the seer, and the seen are all fused together. This is a state of clarity, order, and coherence, and not of an undifferentiated chaos. In the suggestive remark of Meister Eckhart, there is "fusion but not confusion."

The identity of "subject" and "object," which is sometimes called the "supreme identity," is often spoken about in the Upanishadic literature. Identity is a much stronger claim than equality. An equality can arise owing to contingent or incidental factors, but an identity depends on the fundamental nature of the elements involved. When the sages in the Upanishads speak about the identity of Atman and Brahman, they are indicating their discovery about the essential nature of Atman and Brahman, and their oneness. It is not that these two somehow turned out to be the same, but that they are identical by the very nature of reality.

In the description of the supreme identity, the third element in this identity, namely "seeing," is often left out. On the other hand, there is more emphasis on seeing (or pure seeing, or total attention) without the separation of the seer and what is seen, in Buddhism and in the teaching of Krishnamurti. Patañjali also emphasizes the coincidence of all three elements—seeing, the seer, and the seen.

These great utterances of the sages can be helpful reminders of the journey to be traversed and the immense amount of effort needed. These remarks can be a focus for our pondering and meditation. But we should try to avoid mere sloganeering with important ideas which come from the direct perception of the sages unless we can use these formulations as a call and a reminder to search for an experience of these insights. Some harm is done to the profound articulation of the Upanishadic sages if we simply parrot "Atman is Brahman," or, in the context of the teaching of Krishnamurti, if we glibly say that the observer is the observed. We also harm ourselves by imagining and claiming that we have seen the face when we have merely heard the name. We earn some right to use these formulations only when our lips have been cleansed by a burning coal, to use a metaphor from prophet Isaiah.

Perceiver, Perceived, Perceiving

1.42

तत्र शब्दार्थज्ञानविकल्पैः संकीर्णा सवितर्का समापत्तिः

tatra śabda-artha-jñāna-vikalpaiḥ saṃkīrṇā savitarkā samāpattiḥ

Savitarka samapatti is knowledge (*jñana*) based on thought, words and their meaning.

1.43

स्मृतिपरिशुद्धौ स्वरूपशून्येवार्थमात्रनिर्भासा निर्वितर्का

smṛti-pariśuddhau sva-rūpa-śūnya-iva-artha-mātra-nirbhāsā nirvitarkā

Nirvitarka samapatti is knowledge beyond thought, when memory is purified, emptied of its subjectivity, and the object alone shines forth.

1.44

एतयैव सविचारा निर्विचारा च सूक्ष्मविषया व्याख्याता

etayā-eva savichārā nirvichārā cha sūkṣma-viṣayā vyākhyātā

Similarly, subtler *savichara samapatti* (fusion) involving reflection and *nirvichara samapatti*, beyond reflection, are also explained.

1.45

सूक्ष्मविषयत्वं चालिङ्गपर्यवसानम्

sūkṣma-viṣayatvaṃ cha-aliṅga-paryavasānam

The range of subtle objects includes all levels of creation, extending to the limits of the unmanifest.

1.46

ता एव सबीजः समाधिः

tā eva sabījaḥ samādhiḥ

These four levels of samapatti refer to samadhi seeded by external objects (*sabija samadhi*).

Patañjali speaks about four levels of samapatti, all of them leading to a form of samadhi—to insight, presence, attention, or integrated intelligence. These are called *sabija samadhi*, because they are seeded by external objects; that is to say that this kind of samadhi is stimulated by some external object or idea. The four levels of samapatti—savitarka, nirvitarka, savichara, nirvichara—are progressively freer of the thinking and reflective aspects of the mind. In these states, an increasing freedom from subjectivity is achieved. Nirvichara samadhi is a state of attention and intelligence beyond thought, freed from all discursive activity and images.

All levels of samadhi depend upon the capacity and the capability of the mind and refer to the way that all kinds of objects are perceived, from the coarse to the most subtle.

Analogically, the structure of consciousness, which pertains to the levels of samadhi and the transformations (*pariṇama*) which bring about change in these levels, can be likened to the hardware of the mind. The contents of consciousness, the vrittis, correspond to the software of the mind.

The Insight Which Is Full of Order

1.47

निर्विचारवैशारद्येऽध्यात्मप्रसादः

nirvichāra- vaiśāradye' dhyātma-prasādaḥ

Further refinement of nirvichara brings lucidity of the authentic self.

1.48

ऋतम्भरा तत्र प्रज्ञा

ṛtaṃ-bharā tatra prajñā

There, insight is full of order.

1.49

श्रुतानुमानप्रज्ञाभ्यामन्यविषया विशेषार्थत्वात्

śruta-anumāna-prajñābhyām-anya-viṣayā viśeṣā-arthatvāt

The knowledge obtained in this state of consciousness is different from the knowledge obtained by testimony or by inference because of its distinct purpose.

A further refinement of the state of attention beyond thought (*nirvichara*) leads to a state of spiritual lucidity in which the authentic self shines forth without any impressions coming from the outside. Samadhi is not a state of reduced awareness, as is suggested by an occasional translation of "samadhi" as "trance"; instead, it is a state of lucidity, luminosity, and brightness.

As the movements of the mind subside, and as the disturbances caused by the external impressions diminish, the mind dwells in a state of clarity and stillness. The mind becomes emptier and emptier, gaining more and more space. This is closer and closer to the experience of *shunyata*. The doctrine of shunyata developed and flourished in Mahayana Buddhism in India. Shunyata is usually translated as "emptiness," but as Buddhism moved to China, it was more and more understood as "silence," largely owing to the Taoist influences. In a conversation, Roshi Kobori Nanrei, at that time the Head of Rinzai Zen in Japan, remarked that for him the experience of shunyata is best described as "luminosity." Clearly the scholars have much to contribute in our understanding of the subtle realities by clarifying the linguistic usages behind the relevant expressions. But they bring the mind of this world, whereas the sages who have devoted a life-time to a practice with their whole being, including the mind, bring insights from a higher world. A translation provided by a sage needs to be taken seriously even though it may not be "correct" from a linguistic or scholarly point of view.

The words in the sutra (1.48) above, *ritambhara tatra prajña*, are full of mystery. "There, insight is full of order (*rita*)." This is the state of consciousness in which we see things the way they are; not the way we wish them to be or imagine them to be. Any level of consciousness below this level is in the realm of ignorance—more ignorance or less ignorance, but it is not a state of total clarity.

"Rita," related with "ritu" (season), is order. In the Vedas it has the flavor of cosmological or naturalistic order. Later, "rita" gets supplanted by "dharma" which also means order but more often refers to the social order, especially in the Dharma Shastras, such as in the great epic *The Mahabharata*.[6] The very existence and continuation of the earth and heaven depend upon rita. The Rig Veda says, "The whole universe is founded on rita and moves in it"(IV.23.9). Rita is both all pervading and transcendent. The Vedic rita is similar to the ancient Chinese Tao, the mother of all things, and as the Tao Te Ching says, "The Tao that can be spoken of is not the Eternal Tao." Vak, which is said to be the first-born of Rita (Rig Veda I.164.37), is the Word, which was in the Beginning, was with God and was God, and apart from whom nothing came to be (John 1:1-3). In some passages rita and *satya* (truth) are used as synonyms; as are their opposites, *anrita* and *asatya*—for example, in the celebrated mantra *satyameva jayate nanrita*, "Truth alone triumphs, not untruth" (Mundaka Upanishad III.1.6). A part of this mantra, "satyameva jayate," is the epithet used on the official seal of the Government of India.

The insight or the knowledge obtained in the state of ritambhara is completely different from the knowledge obtained by testimony or inference. Knowledge by testimony includes the knowledge from scriptures and the writings of the sages, and knowledge by inference refers to the whole domain of scientific knowledge where all knowledge is based on inference, either by deduction from some premises or by induction from generalizations based upon observations. Thus the knowledge gained in the state of ritambhara is entirely different from what we usually call knowledge. In describing a *sthita prajña* (a person of steady wisdom), Krishna says in the Bhagavad Gita, "When your intelligence will go beyond the whorl of delusion, you will become indifferent to scripture that is heard or that which you have yet to hear. When your intelligence which is bewildered by the revealed scripture will stand unmoving and stable in samadhi, then you will attain to yoga" (2:52-53).

An important aspect of the insight gathered in the state of ritambhara is that it is not an abstraction or a generalization. It is a direct perception of a specific and a unique object in its suchness. A similar point was much emphasized by the visionary poet, William Blake, in his insistence that real insight had to do with the knowledge of what he called "minute particulars." Even God was a Minute Particular for him. In the language of Patañjali (1.24), God is a *purusha vishesha*—unique or particular being. The knowledge in the state of ritambhara is different from scriptural or scientific-philosophic knowledge because of the quality and directness of perception, without mediation by the rational mind; it pertains to minute particulars, not abstract generalizations.

Blaise Pascal, the French mathematician, had a mystical experience in which he had a direct vision of God and he had written "Fire, fire! The God of Abraham, the God of Isaac, the God of Jacob, not that of philosophers and theologians . . ." on a parchment which he had sown into his undershirt in order to keep it close to his heart. The God that Pascal experienced was not the God of Spinoza or Einstein, a God based on theological proofs or philosophical arguments. Such a God does not have the fire or the energy needed to bring about a transformation. What Pascal and the prophets of Judea, and Arjuna in the Bhagavad Gita (chapter 11), experienced was not an abstraction; it was the living God with concreteness, specificity, and power.

The experiences of great visionaries or mystics and prophets—such as Arjuna, Moses, and John of the Cross—are concrete and real, but when they express what they see, they use words which may seem symbolic to us, because what they see is not in our experience. Their description may help us to find a way to a similar experience. However, an experience of a higher-level reality or of subtler materiality requires subtler perception and cognition. Philosophy, science, theology can free us from the lower level concreteness to which we can get excessively attached, but then they can trap us in abstractions, where having heard the name we can imagine having touched the face, mistaking words for reality.

It is very important to prepare ourselves not only to *understand* truth but also to *withstand* it. A glimpse of truth in an unprepared body or mind can shatter the apparatus—just as some drug-induced experiences can. It is difficult to withstand the energy of the *mysterium tremendum.* On seeing the great form of Krishna, Arjuna said, "Although my heart rejoices, my mind is afraid" (BG 11:45). For the well-known physicist, Richard Feynman, a measure of having come upon a great truth was that it created a sense of awe, even terror, in him.

Contemplation Without Seed

1.50

तज्जः संस्कारोऽन्यसंस्कारप्रतिबन्धी

taj-jah saṃskāro' nya-saṃskāra-pratibandhī

The subtle samskaras produced by this knowledge prevent the further accumulation of other impressions.

1.51

तस्यापि निरोधे सर्वनिरोधान्निर्बीजः समाधिः

tasya-api nirodhe sarva-nirodhān-nirbījaḥ samādhiḥ

When even the subtle samskaras have subsided, all movement of the mind ceases and there is contemplation without seed (*nirbija samadhi*).

The state of ritambhara itself produces subtle impressions in the psyche, and these impressions prevent the accumulation of any external impressions, or of the bondage of action according to the law of karma.

Krishnamurti often said that he was not at all influenced by all the training and education he was given, and that his mind remained empty and innocent. That would certainly be the case for someone in the state of silence corresponding to ritambhara—free of the past, not by forgetting but by remaining in a state free from the effects of conditioning.

A state of perfect samadhi, seedless contemplation, is reached when even the impressions of the ritambhara state have subsided. This is a state of presence or attention without stimulation from any external object. It is pure seeing without the separation of the seer and the seen. Whatever one attends to is seen in its suchness, the thing in itself, without any subjectivity introduced by the categories of the mind. Using a felicitous phrase of Plotinus, then one is in a flight from the alone to the Alone.

Endnotes:

1 In this connection, the readers' attention is drawn to an article "Is Religion Psychotherapy?" in *The Spiritual Roots of Yoga*.

2 Hujwiri in R.A. Nicholoson, *The Kashf al-Mahjub: The Oldest Persian Treatise on Sufism.* London, Luzac, 1911, p. 39.

3 Soren Kierkegaard, "Man's Need of God Constitutes his Highest Perfection" in *Edifying Discourses.* New York: Fontana Books, 1958, p. 151.

4 In this connection, please see the article "Is the Everlasting Eternal?", in *The Spiritual Roots of Yoga*.

5 For an understanding of the teaching of Sri Anirvan, two books are highly recommended: Lizelle Reymond and Sri Anirvan, *To Live Within* and Sri Anirvan, *Inner Yoga.*

6 For a further discussion of this concept, please see "Sacrifice and Order: Yoga, Rita and Yajña" in *The Spiritual Roots of Yoga.*

Sadhana Pada

▪

Practice

The Forces of Hindrance

The Practice of Yoga

2.1

तपः स्वाध्यायेश्वरप्रणिधानानि क्रियायोगः

tapaḥ svādhyāya-īśvara-praṇidhānāni kriyā-yogaḥ

The practice of yoga consists of self-discipline (*tapas*), self-study (*svadhyaya*), and dedication to Ishvara.

It is also possible to translate the sutra above as "Tapas, svadhyaya, and dedication to Ishvara constitute Kriya Yoga." In this way of looking at this sutra, Kriya Yoga is a separate yoga, even the most distinctive yoga to be associated with Patañjali. However more simply, "kriya yoga" literally means the activity of yoga and reminds us once again of the need to engage in the practice of yoga.

"Tapas" is sometimes translated as "effort," "austerity" or "asceticism," as well as "self-discipline." It includes a reference to the heat which is generated with intense effort. Self-discipline is absolutely crucial in any practice of yoga. The whole of our psychosomatic organism needs to be rightly ordered. The lower, which is to say less conscious, parts in us need to be disciplined by the higher parts and brought to function with the understanding coming from above. Otherwise, good ideas and resolutions amount to nothing if the parts which have to carry out these resolutions refuse to cooperate. As Madame de Salzmann said, "The body needs to be disciplined—punished or rewarded—not tortured. It must learn to obey something higher. The body needs to be available."

Self-study (*svadhyaya*) is emphasized in the whole of the Indian tradition. Any of our manifestations, such as the tone of voice, gesture, posture, attitude to myself or to parents or to others, are fit subjects for self-observation which can reveal more and more of ourselves and clarify deeper tensions and motivations. Self-study may begin as a study of very personal and quite particular likes and dislikes, but very soon we discover that self-study is in fact a study of the human condition as it is expressed in our individual situations.

The deeper the level of the self of our study, the more deeply do we approach the generality of the human situation in all human beings. All the sages in India have asserted that our deepest self, Atman, is identically the same as the highest Universal Self, Brahman, and that the highest reality dwells in the deepest part of every individual. With a similar insight, Meister Eckhart said that our soul is as infinite as God.

In approaching self-study we need to ask what levels of the self need to be known and also what the level of the self that knows is. The answer to these questions will vary at different stages of the study. At the beginning, we gather data about ourselves, and begin to see patterns of behavior. Our own particular desires and fears and our specific ambitions, mostly arising out of our conditioning, will become evident. Gradually, we begin to see that fear and desire are universal characteristics of human beings, although in each case manifesting in particular ways. We begin to understand that the whole of humanity is run by forces of reward and punishment, by the wish for approval and a fear of disapproval—from parents, from the society, from traditions, from God. We also begin to see that below the layer of fear and ambition, there is an aspiration for a connection with the Source of all life and meaning. In moments of insight, we realize that we are both the searchers and the objects of our search. Ultimately, of course, as the Bhagavad Gita says, the Self knows the Self by Itself. "Not I, the I that I am, know these things," says the Christian mystic Boehme, "but God knows them in me."

"Svadhyaya" is sometimes translated as "a study of sacred literature." However, there is no meaning to a study of the sacred literature unless it leads to an impartial observation of our selves, more and more deeply and more and more clearly. A repeated emphasis of the sacred literature in

India is on self-knowledge. Self-knowledge is an essential step towards an identity with God, because deep down there is a particle of divinity dwelling in each of us. Krishna repeatedly says in the Bhagavad Gita that he, the highest God, is seated in the heart of everyone. Even though the canonical books of the Bible do not emphasize self-knowledge, Christ says in the Gospel of Thomas, "The Kingdom is inside you, and it is outside you. When you come to know yourselves, then you will become known, and you will realize that it is you who are the sons of the living Father. But if you will not know yourselves, you live in poverty, and you are poverty" (II, 2:3).

Dedication to Ishvara, God, is the other practice suggested here. (In this connection, also see sutra 1.23.) Following a universal traditional idea that the human microcosmos can in principle reflect the entire large cosmos, the deepest part of oneself—the part which is beyond Prakriti, which is "unaffected by suffering, by action, by fruits of action or by subliminal intentions," as is said in the sutra 1.24—is Ishvara, the primordial and eternal teacher. The three practices—self-discipline, self-study, and dedication to God—are intimately connected with each other; one is not possible without the other.

2.2

समाधिभावनार्थः क्लेशतनुकरणार्थश्च

samādhi-bhāvana-arthaḥ kleśa-tanū-karaṇa-arthaś-cha

Yoga is for cultivating samadhi and for weakening the hindrances (*kleshas*).

Here the purpose of yoga is defined differently, and somewhat more positively, than in the first chapter where it was said that yoga is the stopping of the movements of the mind. The purpose of yoga is now said to be the weakening of hindrances to the attainment of samadhi—the state of insightful attention in a totally still mind. It was partly in anticipation of the present sutra that sutra 1.2 was rendered as "Yoga is establishing the mind in stillness."

Patañjali then proceeds to enumerate the various hindrances (*kleshas*) to samadhi.

Hindrances

2.3

अविद्यास्मितारागद्वेषाभिनिवेशाः क्लेशाः

avidyā-asmitā-rāga-dveṣa-abhiniveśāḥ kleśāḥ

The kleshas are ignorance (*avidya*), the sense of a separate self (*asmita*), attraction (*raga*), aversion (*dvesha*), and clinging to the status quo (*abhinivesha*).

2.4

अविद्याक्षेत्रमुत्तरेषां प्रसुप्ततनुविच्छिन्नोदाराणाम्

avidyā kṣetram-uttareṣāṃ prasupta-tanu-vichchhinna-udārāṇām

Avidya is the cause of all the others, whether dormant, attenuated, intermittent, or fully active.

2.5

अनित्याशुचिदुःखानात्मसु नित्यशुचिसुखात्मख्यातिरविद्या

anitya-aśuchi-duḥkha-anātmasu nitya-śuchi-sukha-ātma-khyātir-avidyā

Avidya is seeing the transient as eternal, the impure as pure, dissatisfaction as pleasure, the non-Self as Self.

Several hindrances are enumerated here—avidya, asmita, raga, dvesha, and abhinivesha—but the root cause of all of these kleshas is ignorance. This is so according to all the sages in India: the basic source of our human predicament is ignorance of our own true nature and of the nature of the cosmos. Everything else follows from this. "*Avijja parmam malam* (ignorance is the great blemish)," is a remark of the Buddha in the Dhammapada. It is in ignorance that we mistake the transient for the eternal, the unsatisfactory as satisfactory, and the non-Self as Self. All this leads to illusion, conflict and suffering, to be free of which is the aim of yoga.

Since the root cause of the problem is ignorance, naturally, the solution is jñana, knowledge. As was already said (see 1.49), this knowledge is a radically different kind than the scientific or philosophic or scriptural knowledge. There are several words to refer to this special kind of knowledge: *vidya* (cognate with the English "video", to see), *jñana* (cognate with "gnosis"), *bodhi* (the root, *budh*, of which is the same as in "buddha," awake and discerning), *prajña* (insight). This insightful and direct perception is possible only when the mind is in samadhi, a state of consciousness in which there is a non-fluctuating and steady attention so that the perceiving, the perceiver, and the perceived are fused into one single ordered whole. When the hindrances to the state of samadhi are removed, true insight into the nature of reality results.

2.6

दृगदर्शनशक्त्योरेकात्मतेवास्मिता

dṛg-darśana-śaktyor-eka-ātmatā-iva-asmitā

Asmita is the misidentification of the power of seeing with what is seen.

2.7

सुखानुशयी रागः

sukha-anuśayī rāgaḥ

Raga arises from dwelling on pleasant experiences.

2.8

दुःखानुशयी द्वेषः

duḥkha-anuśayī dveṣaḥ

Dvesha arises from clinging to unpleasant experiences.

2.9

स्वरसवाही विदुषोऽपि तथारूढोऽभिनिवेशः

sva-rasa-vāhī viduṣo' pi tathā rūḍho' bhiniveśaḥ

Abhinivesha is the automatic tendency for continuity; it overwhelms even the wise.

Asmita, the notion that I am a separate self, isolated from the whole, with my own ego-centered projects, is the first product of avidya. "Asmita" literally means "I am this" or "I am that," thus separating the small self from the entire vast reservoir of Being, from Brahman (literally, The Vastness). The Self says "I AM"—as in the very grand sayings of Christ, especially in the Gospel of John, in which he says in the state of oneness with Yahweh (which in Hebrew means "I AM"), I AM is the way and the truth and the life[1]—but the ego says "I am this" or "I am that," thus attaching itself only to a small portion of the Vastness. Asmita is the result of the misidentification of the power of seeing, which is Purusha (or Atman), with what is seen, namely chitta. Contrary to William Blake's reminder that "Perception is not limited by the organs of perception," the isolated self identifies itself increasingly with the mind or with the body, seeing the vehicle (body-mind) as the self. In the movement from asmita (I am this) to *Soham* (I AM), from a limited self to the Self, from the identification with chitta to oneness with Purusha, from the self-will of Arjuna to his willingness to carry out Krishna's will, the right order is discovered. The resulting insight is naturally full of truth and order (*rita*), as an earlier sutra said, "ritambhara tatra prajña" (1.48).

Raga is the attachment to pleasure; dvesha is the attachment to suffering. The natural tendency to wish to relive pleasurable experiences is understandable, but it is particularly odd that we are more attached to our suffering than to our pleasures. Moments of humiliation or situations in which we were ridiculed or made to feel small come back to us much more frequently and with a larger emotional force than the moments in which we were admired or looked up to. Experiences of suffering, especially psychological suffering, create deep grooves in our psyche, drawing attention to themselves quite mechanically and frequently. Nations and groups can be attached to past humiliations and sufferings, perpetuating a sense of victimization from generation to generation. No wonder that, among many other definitions of yoga in the Bhagavad Gita, Krishna says that "yoga is the breaking of the bond with suffering" (6:23).

Freedom from the whole domain of like-dislike, and pleasure-pain is a very great freedom. Then we do what needs to be done, whether we like it or not. It is possible to say that the whole meaning of the exquisite symbol of the cross for a serious Christian lies precisely in this: even if something is disagreeable or unpleasant or will produce pain, if it is necessary according to a higher understanding, then one would embrace the suffering intentionally and submit oneself to the right action. The outstanding example of this is the Christ himself. On the eve of his crucifixion, he prayed to God in the Garden of Gethsemane, "Father, if it is possible, let this cup pass me by. Yet not my will but thine be done" (Mark 14:36).

Although "abhinivesha" is sometimes translated as "a wish to live," it is closer to "a wish to continue," or "a wish to preserve the status quo."Abhinivesha is what is technically called "inertia" in physics, as in Newton's First Law of Motion (also called the Law of Inertia) according to which a body continues in a state of rest or of motion in a straight line unless acted upon by an external force. Abhinivesha is the wish for continuity of any state and any situation, because it is known. We fear the unknown and therefore we fear change which may lead to the unknown. In fact, this fear is of a discontinuation of the known, simply because the unknown, if it is truly unknown, cannot produce fear or pleasure. In one of the dialogues of Plato, there is a scene in which Socrates has been given hemlock to drink and he is about to die. Some of his disciples are quite understandably very upset and are crying. Socrates says to them, "You are behaving as if you know what happens at death. And furthermore, as if you know that what happens is undesirable. As for me, I do not know. Therefore, I am free."

Freedom from abhinivesha, from the wish to continue the known, is a dying to the self, or a dying to the world, which is so much spoken about in so many traditions. It has often been said by the sages that only when we are willing and able to die to our old self, can we be born into a new vision and a new life. There is a cogent remark of St. Paul: "I die daily" (1 Corinthians 15:31). A profound saying of an ancient Sufi master, echoed in so much of sacred literature, says, "If you die before you die, then you do not die when you die." During a conversation about life after death, Krishnamurti said, "The real question is 'Can I die while I am living? Can I die to all my collections—material, psychological, religious?' If you can die to all that, then you'll find out what is there after death. Either there is nothing; absolutely nothing. Or there *is* something. But you cannot find out until you actually die while living."

Dying daily is a spiritual practice—a regaining of a sort of innocence, which is quite different from ignorance, akin to openness and humility. It is an active unknowing; not achieved but needing to be renewed again and again. All serious meditation is a practice of dying to the ordinary self. If we allow ourselves the luxury of not knowing, and if we are not completely full of ourselves, we can hear the subtle whispers under the noises of the world outside and inside ourselves. Sri Anirvan remarked that the whole world is like a big bazaar in which everyone is shouting at the top of their voice wanting to make their little bargain. A recognition of this can invite us to true metanoia, a turning around, to a new way of being. Otherwise, abhinivesha, the wish which maintains the status quo, persists.

This wish for continuity is rooted in a search for security and for permanence. Abhinivesha, the wish to hold onto the past, keeps us in the momentum of time. Being present from moment to moment requires a freedom from abhinivesha, and a freedom from abhinivesha brings us to a radiant presence, where we can be free of the fear of dying and of living.

Freedom from abhinivesha is intimately related with the Buddhist understanding of *anitya* ("*anichcha*" in Pali): nothing is permanent and therefore change is the norm of the cosmos. Noting that the Tao is transformation, a Taoist sage said, "Ride the chariots of the Tao." Transformation is said to be the fundamental principle of the cosmos. Fire, Agni, is the principal symbol of transformation and is invoked as a priest. No Hindu ceremony—whether name giving, initiation into schooling, marriage or funeral—is complete without the presence of fire as a witness. The very first mantra of the Rig Veda, the most ancient text in any Indo-European language, is an invocation of Agni.

> *Om! agnimile purohitam*
> *yajñasya devam ritvijam (Rig Veda I.1.1)*
>
> *Om! I invoke Agni, the first Priest,*
> *the lord of yajña, born of Order . . .*

The vrittis and the kleshas both prevent a quiet and a steady attention, but there are subtle differences between them. The vrittis, the distractions of the mind, are personal and particular for each one of us, while the kleshas are cosmological forces which constitute the psychological reality of ordinary humanity. Freedom from the vrittis can be achieved by finding a freedom from the noise within, possible with our own effort, but freedom from the kleshas is the result of a transformation of the ordinary level of the mind and this requires an internal reordering in the light of a higher mind. Freedom from the vrittis is possible for the Son of Man, but only the Son of God can find a freedom from the kleshas. With dedication to Ishvara, we acknowledge that without a connection to the larger cosmos and to the higher levels of reality we remain isolated and imprisoned in our own smallness.

Vrittis are a result of human conditioning—which varies from person to person—but the kleshas are a result of the human condition to which we are all subject. Efforts to be free of both the vrittis and the kleshas require a sacrifice of our smallness and of our attachment to the way we are. What is needed is a dying to the old self, in order to allow a new birth, a spiritual birth.

Freedom from Hindrances

2.10

ते प्रतिप्रसवहेयाः सूक्ष्माः

te pratiprasava-heyāḥ sūkṣmāḥ

These subtle kleshas can be overcome by reversing the natural flow (*pratiprasava*) and returning to the source.

2.11

ध्यानहेयास्तद् वृत्तयः

dhyāna-heyās-tad-vṛttayaḥ

Their effects can be reduced by meditation (*dhyana*).

The dynamic principle of Prakriti expresses itself as an externalizing force through the force of creation and manifestation. The inherent movement of Prakriti is that of pravritti, an outward centrifugal tendency, which moves further and further away from the center where the Source of all creation is. The counter force is that of nivritti, an inward centripetal movement which seeks the center. Yoga is, as is all spiritual teaching, for making a connection with the source of life; therefore its movement is against the automatic flow of nature. As a fact of our human condition (as in the Christian doctrine of "original sin"), we are all heirs to the unrefined state of prakrita. To be transformed into a refined or sanskrita being requires art, skill, education—in other words, this transformation requires yoga.

Pratiprasava, the reversal of the natural flow, is required. It is the reversal of the natural outward tendencies of Prakriti. Since the usual tendency of the whole of creation, therefore also of our mind, is outward, in order to move towards the center a reversal is needed, a turning around, a metanoia. It is also possible to say that spiritual practice, yoga, although opposed to the lower nature (or animal nature) in human beings, is in harmony with our higher nature (or spiritual nature). What we ordinarily regard as natural is what is usual and habitual with us. Our automatic habitual postures, thoughts, and feelings are manifestations of our ordinary state of consciousness, a state of sleep or of mechanicality. It is through an impartial self-study (svadhyaya) that we become aware of the enormous strength of these tendencies which we need to struggle against as a part of self-discipline (tapas).

We can appreciate the force of the tendencies of our lower ordinary nature during meditation where the distracted nature of our mind which runs after one association and then another is obvious. As we persist in abhyasa, we can gradually acquire an attitude of detachment (vairagya) towards these distractions. As we identify ourselves less and less with these tendencies, realizing that they do not represent our real identity, we can become freer and freer of them. The force of the kleshas can diminish in meditation as we practice dying to our ordinary, habitual self, and orient ourselves to deeper aspects of our being.

2.12

क्लेशमूलः कर्माशयो दृष्टादृष्टजन्मवेदनीयः

kleśa-mūlaḥ karma-āśayo dṛṣṭa-adṛṣṭa-janma-vedanīyaḥ

Past actions, rooted in kleshas, give rise to experiences in present or future births.

2.13

सति मूले तद्विपाको जात्यायुर्भोगाः

sati mūle tad-vipāko jāty-āyur-bhogāḥ

As long as the root exists, the effects will be experienced as birth and in the quality and duration of life.

2.14

ते ह्लादपरितापफलाः पुण्यापुण्यहेतुत्वात्

te hlāda-paritāpa-phalāḥ puṇya-apuṇya-hetutvāt

Joy is the result of right action, sorrow of wrong action.

Every action leaves an impression on our being, and the quality of our being predisposes us towards certain sorts of action. This is the law of karma. Although this law applies to all creatures and things, if we confine our attention to human beings, we can express the law of karma as follows: as one is, so one acts; and as one acts, so one becomes. In the mutually interactive system of action and being, according to the law of karma, being affects action and action affects being.

If I am a certain kind of person, I naturally find myself doing certain sorts of actions. In turn, the actions that I perform or the events that affect me, leave grooves on my being and produce tendencies which make me a different kind of person. At the next opportunity, I will act in accordance with these tendencies of my being, and in this way my future action (karma) is determined by my past actions. Major events leave deep impressions in the psyche, creating knots in it that affect our future actions for a long time without our necessarily being aware of the knots or of their initial causes.

As a general principle, the effects of karma are not restricted to only one lifetime; the law cuts across the boundary of what is ordinarily called life and death. Action here does not mean simply physical activity, but also includes thoughts and feelings and intentions. If we think hateful thoughts about someone, not only does that reflect the quality of our being, but it also further affects the quality of our being.

The law of karma is an example of a traditional law of nature as understood by the Hindus and the Buddhists. This law is a law of determinism; but it is also a law that makes freedom possible and provides the basis for any spiritual practice. Understood partially, from the point of view of only one level within a human being, the law of karma creates a closed circle from which no one can escape, and it has quite often been understood in this manner, leading to despair and resignation. However, when viewed from the perspective of a whole person, the law of karma can indicate to those willing to undertake the discipline involved in the cleansing of their perceptions, precisely what the knots are in their lives that compel them to act the way they do, even against the will and understanding of their right mind, and how to resolve and overcome these knots.

More importantly, a person can depend on the law of karma and undertake a spiritual striving in the assurance of the knowledge that the universe or the gods do not act capriciously and that no one is elevated or degraded accidentally. Each one of us is responsible for our life—even to the extent of salvation or perdition—and the dignity of our human existence and action is founded on the solidity of a law working in every part of the cosmos.

In correspondence with our own deep-seated spiritual urges, each one of us has the possibility of making efforts in order to overcome the compulsions of the lawful and natural workings of our tendencies, which are based on our past experiences, knowledge, and impressions. This is the meaning of spiritual striving, a struggle against our own determined nature and conditioning. It is useful to remember that our struggle is in the midst of large forces; the spiritual aspects of the cosmos help our own spiritual endeavors, just as the mechanical or downward cosmological forces aid our downward tendencies.

As the sutras above state, all our experiences in this life are the result of past tendencies and actions, which have been rooted in the kleshas, just as future births and experiences will be determined by the undertakings in this life. Happiness and sorrow result from right and wrong actions. However, Krishna reminds us in the Bhagavad Gita, "You have the right to action, but only to action, never to its fruits. Let not the fruits of your works be your motive, neither let there be any attachment to inaction. Firm in yoga engage in actions, having abandoned attachment, having become equable to success and failure, O Arjuna, for equanimity is yoga" (2:47-48).

Yoga for the Ending of Sorrow

2.15

परिणामतापसंस्कारदुःखैर्गुणवृत्तिविरोधाच्च दुःखमेव सर्वं विवेकिनः

pariṇāma-tāpa-saṃskāra-duḥkhair-guṇa-vṛtti-virodhāch-cha duḥkham-eva sarvaṃ vivekinaḥ

For the discerning, all is sorrow, resulting from the mismatch between what is actual and what is thought, and because of the suffering inherent in change, pain, and from past conditioning.

2.16

हेयं दुःखमनागतम्

heyaṃ duḥkham-anāgatam

Future suffering is to be avoided.

The fact of suffering (*dukkha*) cannot be denied. That there is suffering is the First Noble Truth of the Buddha. For the Buddha, the cause of suffering is *tanha*, selfish desire or simply selfishness. For Patañjali, the source of suffering is the mismatch between the way it actually is, determined by the interaction of the gunas, the forces and constituents of Prakriti, and what the mind thinks and expects, shaped by the vrittis. The gulf between reality and thought leads to sorrow. In our life, this gap is most manifest in our expectations of ourselves and of other people and our actual experience.

For the existentialist philosophers, who assume that the mind is the knower of reality, the recognition of the fact that reality does not correspond to thought led to the conclusion that the universe is absurd. This assumption is strenuously denied by all of Indian philosophy, and in any case by Patañjali for whom the mind is an instrument of knowledge. The real knower is Purusha who knows through the mind and not with the mind. Purusha alone can know reality, and only when the mind is completely free of the vrittis can it act as a perfect instrument of knowledge. Then we do not have expectations about the world and about others, we see and accept reality as it is.

Because of the consequences of the force of abhinivesha (see 2.9), the klesha which causes us to wish to continue in the state which is known, we suffer when there is a possibility of change. But change is constant. The universe is dynamic, constantly subject to the force of time: we move from one place to another; we see the seasons change and the movement of the planets; we grow old; we die. Even when pleasure exists, the very impermanence of pleasure leads to sorrow. There are instances of pain, and sorrowful consequences of past experiences which are rooted in all the kleshas. Therefore, for the discerning, dukkha is a pervasive feature of life.

As the very next sutra indicates, this realistic assessment is not a doctrine of pessimism. Patañjali is not simply saying that future suffering can be avoided, but exhorts us to take up the challenge, to undertake the practice of yoga so that ignorance can be removed and therefore all the kleshas and the suffering arising from them can be overcome.

▪ The Seer and the Seen

2.17

द्रष्टृदृश्ययोः संयोगो हेयहेतुः

draṣṭṛ-dṛśyayoḥ saṃyogo heya-hetuḥ

The cause of suffering is the misidentification of the seer with the seen.

2.18

प्रकाशक्रियास्थितिशीलं भूतेन्द्रियात्मकं भोगापवर्गार्थं दृश्यम्

prakāśa-kriyā-sthiti-śīlaṃ bhūta-indriya-ātmakaṃ bhoga-apavarga-arthaṃ dṛśyam

The seen consists of material elements and the sense organs. These have qualities of clarity, activity, and stability. The seen exists to serve the aims of experience and liberation.

2.19

विशेषाविशेषलिङ्गमात्रालिङ्गानि गुणपर्वाणि

viśeṣa-aviśeṣa-liṅga-mātra-aliṅgāni guṇa-parvāṇi

Everything that exists, whether particular, general, manifest, or unmanifest is constituted by the gunas, the fundamental qualities of nature.

Patañjali emphasizes that suffering or dissatisfaction is caused by the misidentification of the seer with the seen. The suggestion is not that the coming together of the seer and the seen—that is, of Purusha and Prakriti—causes suffering. This has unfortunately been sometimes suggested as the meaning of Patañjali's teaching. According to this interpretation, the aim of yoga becomes a complete separation of Purusha from Prakriti. As is clear from the sutras above and the ones to follow, Prakriti exists for the sake of Purusha, and provides the opportunity both for experience and liberation (2.18, 21). Prakriti does not have any purpose of its own; it exists only for the sake of Purusha. Sorrow arises when the one is mistaken for the other because of ignorance. The solution is not the separation of Purusha and Prakriti but the right cognizance of their roles.

The whole realm of the seen, Prakriti, is the *kshetra* (field), and the seer, Purusha, is the *kshetrajña* (knower of the field). The field is the domain of cause and effect, and the knower of the field belongs to an altogether different dimension, that of awareness. In the Bhagavad Gita, Krishna says, "Know me as the knower of the field in all fields. True knowledge consists in knowing the field and the knower of the field . . . Prakriti is said to be the origin of cause and effect and the sense of agency; Purusha is said to be the origin of the experiences of pleasure and pain. Purusha seated in Prakriti enjoys the gunas born of Prakriti . . . the Witness, the Consenter, the Sustainer, the Enjoyer, the almighty Lord and supreme Self, thus is called Purusha in the body" (13:2, 20-22).

All of Prakriti, at all levels of manifestation, from the coarsest to the subtlest, is constituted by the three gunas, three qualities and forces. The three gunas are *sattva*, *rajas*, and *tamas*. Each of these qualities can be expressed at all levels from the most negative to the most positive. At best, sattva is clarity, purity, mindfulness, contentment; but at a lower level this can lead to indifference and passivity. In its positive manifestation, rajas is activity, exploration, and effort; but at a lower level this can lead to agitation and grasping. Tamas is the force of stability; but at a lower level this can lead to inertia and heedlessness. "Neither on earth, nor in heaven among the gods, is there a being that is free from the working of the three gunas, born of Prakriti. From sattva, jñana is born; from rajas, greed; from tamas, proceed negligence and delusion, also ignorance" (BG 18:40; 14:17).

2.20

द्रष्टा दृशिमात्रः शुद्धोऽपि प्रत्ययानुपश्यः

draṣṭā dṛśi-mātraḥ śuddho' pi pratyaya-anupaśyaḥ

The Seer is only the power of pure seeing. Although pure, the Seer appears to see with the mind.

2.21

तदर्थ एव दृश्यस्यात्मा

tad-artha eva dṛśyasya-ātmā

The seen is for the sake of the Seer.

Purusha, the Seer, only sees. Seeing is the only characteristic or property of Purusha. By itself it is pure seeing, but it manifests its vision through the categories and the qualities of the mind. Therefore a purification of the mind is required so that it could be a proper instrument without introducing any particularity or subjectivity.

This Seer—Purusha, Conscious Energy, Transcendent Being—sees at every level of manifestation of Prakriti. It is not located at a singular point somewhere outside Prakriti. The whole vertical axis of awareness, orthogonal to the material manifestation of Prakriti represented by the horizontal plane, shares in the being of Purusha. Along this vertical axis of Conscious Energy, of consciring, of seeing, we can see more and more clearly and impartially as our organs of perception are cleansed and the vrittis and the kleshas are diminished. Purusha is only the witnessing consciousness, or *sakshi bhava*. For Purusha to act, it must be associated with Prakriti. The necessity of this relationship is expressed by Ishvarakrishna, the author of *Samkhyakarika*, when he points out that Purusha without Prakriti is lame and Prakriti without Purusha is blind.

Sometimes, it is possible to submit the visible, the whole realm of Prakriti, for the power to see. In that submission the right order between Purusha and Prakriti, between Conscious Energy and matter, is found. The right relationship cannot be found if one part of the relationship is discarded.

Patañjali speaks in terms of Purusha and Prakriti; this can appear like an excessively abstract philosophical principle. But because there is an isomorphism between *brahmanda* (macrocosmos) and *kshudra brahmanda* (microcosmos), we can recognize that the same relationship exists within us. The relationship between the spirit and our body, or between the higher and more conscious energy—which is in the body but is not of the body—and the body-mind, is a necessary one. The Real I, the Atman (the Self) and an individual self, *jiva* which includes the whole psychosomatic complex, need to be rightly related. Madame de Salzmann so much emphasized that the higher energy has to make a contact with the body:

> *The body has to serve something else, not itself. The body itself is designed for destruction; it has to serve something else.*

This does not mean that the human incarnation is not necessary. As she continues,

> *One need not change what one is. But what is this for? All this, all of one's life and activities, are not for oneself, but for something else. They are for the sake of the higher energy. The body is necessary, but it is not the most important thing. It must obey something else. In fact, the body wants and likes the contact with the energy which comes from above, which comes from God. But we are taken by automatism. One must liberate the subtle body from the prison of habits of the ordinary body.*

Freedom from Ignorance

2.22

कृतार्थं प्रति नष्टमप्यनष्टं तदन्यसाधारणत्वात्

kṛta-arthaṃ prati naṣṭam-apy-anaṣṭaṃ tad-anya-sādhā-raṇatvāt

Having served its purpose, for one who is liberated, the phenomenal world no longer appears as before, but it continues as such for others.

2.23

स्वस्वामिशक्त्योः स्वरूपोपलब्धिहेतुः संयोगः

sva-svāmi-śaktyoḥ sva-rūpa-upalabdhi-hetuḥ saṃyogaḥ

The connection between the Seer and the seen causes a mistaken perception of identity between the force of the visible and the power to see.

2.24

तस्य हेतुरविद्या

tasya hetur-avidyā

The cause of this is ignorance (*avidya*).

Prakriti, the phenomenal world, does not disappear for a realized yogi. The world is not an illusion or a dream or a nightmare from which the yogi needs to wake up. The world exists and its reality and its bewitchment continue to be experienced by others. But for one who realizes the Self, is freed from the allurements of the world and is asleep to its temptations, the ordinary world acquires a dreamlike quality. To use a classical metaphor, "a sage is like a dead man walking." The world is no longer fascinating or bewitching for a liberated person.

There is a persistent tendency in Indian thought, especially in the ascetic tradition, to denigrate the world of space and time and the world of matter and energy. For people with such an attitude, it seems as if the world is a mistake, and the chief purpose of our existence is to undo the world and life, in order to merge into the undifferentiated ocean of consciousness. This point of view would suggest that those who have attained enlightenment can exit the world because they have nothing left to do. Such an attitude can only be a terrible misunderstanding. Enlightenment has no meaning unless it is accompanied by compassion. In fact, we would recognize those who have reached a higher level of understanding by their compassion. Such beings are quite aware of the suffering of humanity and of other creatures, and they do their best, directly or indirectly through their followers, to alleviate suffering. The Bodhisattvas take the remarkable vow that they will continue being reincarnated again and again to help suffering creatures until every blade of grass is enlightened.

We have a very helpful reminder from Krishna that we are responsible for the maintenance of order (*dharma*) in the world and among people: "It is not possible for an embodied being to entirely abandon action; but one who gives up the attachment to fruits of action is a true renouncer (*tyagi*). Even though there is nothing in the three worlds that I need to do, nor is there anything that I have to gain, I engage in action. If I do not engage ceaselessly in action, all these worlds will perish. Those who know do not act with attachment to the fruits of action; those who know should act without attachment" (BG 18:11; 3:22-25).

The world would not exist if Purusha and Prakriti were completely separated from each other. Purusha is what vivifies and animates Prakriti as the breath of God animates the human body. What is important, and Patañjali emphasizes this point again and again, is not to confuse Purusha with Prakriti, or Spirit with the body. This misidentification is rooted in ignorance and leads to illusion and suffering.

2.25

तदभावात्संयोगाभावो हानं तद्दृशेः कैवल्यम्

tad-abhāvāt saṃyoga-abhāvo hānaṃ tad-dṛśeḥ kaivalyam

With the disappearance of ignorance, the misidentification no longer exists. Then pure seeing alone remains.

2.26

विवेकख्यातिरविप्लवा हानोपायः

viveka-khyātir-aviplavā hāna-upāyaḥ

Steady vision of discernment (*viveka*) is the way to overcome ignorance.

2.27

तस्य सप्तधा प्रान्तभूमिः प्रज्ञा

tasya saptadhā prānta-bhūmiḥ prajñā

Wisdom (*prajña*) is accomplished in seven stages.

Ignorance, the source of suffering, consists in the misidentification of Prakriti with Purusha, and can be removed by viveka, right discernment. Viveka is the highest virtue in Indian spirituality. It may seem that the Bhakti tradition of spirituality regards love as the highest virtue rather than viveka. On the face of it, viveka and love may seem far apart, but as has been remarked upon by many sages, the driving force of higher love (*parabhakti*, in the language of the Bhagavad Gita) is the recognition that what calls us and what attracts us at our depth, is not what we know. What we most love is not what we know, but what knows us and draws us; and a constant vigilance, a steady discernment, is needed in order to be mindful of what is Ultimately Real and what is below that. It is the love for the subtler realities which drives us to be clearer and clearer about those realities.

The only one thing which is needed is to remember that God exists and that we exist under His gaze. The only practice that is needed is the practice of the presence of God. Everything else follows from that one thing. The Christian classic of spirituality, *The Cloud of Unknowing*, is one of the best illustrations of this point of view. We are situated in the middle of two clouds. These are two domains, two atmospheres of being—one below us and the other above. Below us is the "cloud of forgetting," the subjective cloud which needs to be formed by us and needs to be expanded so that it could contain the whole creation, everything other than God. We need to practice placing more and more things in this cloud so we can rise above them. But the things of the world, or of worldliness, keep asserting themselves again and again. The aim here is to put the whole of creation, the whole of Prakriti, coarse and subtle, in the cloud of forgetting. This includes everything we call ourselves. To forget ourselves and the world is to place all this in the cloud of forgetting. This is the consummate practice of vairagya. Nothing else is worth remembering except God. The cloud of forgetting is the domain of total self-forgetfulness. That is the highest vairagya, freedom from selfishness, which is the same as freedom from myself.

> *Just as the* cloud of unknowing *lies above you, between you and your God, so you must fashion a* cloud of forgetting *beneath you, between you and every created thing.* (The Cloud of Unknowing, *p. 53)*

The "cloud of unknowing" is the one domain which needs to be penetrated if one wishes to come to God who is on the other side of this cloud or above it. This cloud is objective, existing by itself and forever. It is not something we need to fashion, but we need to penetrate it. The attitude which is essential here is of unknowing—not ignorance but innocence. "The wisdom of the wise is folly in the eyes of God," says St. Paul (1 Corinthians 3:19). The true religious mind is silent, free of fear and self-importance, innocent, open, and vulnerable.

> *Thought cannot comprehend God. And so, I prefer to abandon all I can know, choosing rather to love him whom I cannot know. Though we cannot know him, we can love him. By love he may be touched and embraced, never by thought. (*The Cloud of Unknowing, *p. 54)*

Love for God is a love for something we do not know, but we are drawn to. This is true for us at all levels of love; we do not know rationally why we love. I participated in several small group discussions with Krishnamurti, and sometimes I could not understand why he gave so little importance to making efforts, to undertaking practice, and to thought. On one occasion, there must have been some exasperation in my voice. He stopped me in mid-sentence, and asked: "But sir why do you keep coming?" Without the intervention of any thought or hesitation, I said, "Because I love you." This was the truth of the matter. One does not know why one does certain things but there is an interaction of subtle forces, inside as well as outside, and in matters of love or spiritual influences, there is a mutuality of relationship. Does an iron filing decide to be attracted to a magnet? Does it know why? As long as we are making decisions we are not following the heart. The heart chooses without an enumeration of mental reasons which can give a satisfactory explanation to somebody else.

Love for God is at the heart of *The Cloud of Unknowing*. "He whom neither men nor angels can grasp by knowledge can be embraced by love." (*The Book of Privy Counseling,* by the same author, p. 50). But "whatever we may say of it [love] it is not it, but only about it." (p.169, *ibid.*)

> *And so stand firmly and avoid pitfalls, keep to the path you are on. Let your longing relentlessly beat up the* cloud of unknowing *that lies between you and your God. Pierce that cloud with the keen shaft of your love, spurn the thought of anything less than God." (*The Cloud of Unknowing, *p. 63)*

Through a steady practice of discernment we can learn to distinguish between the real and the unreal, between Purusha and Prakriti, between the Self and non-Self. Towards one a searcher needs to cultivate vairagya, and place it in the cloud of forgetting; towards the other, which is beyond the cloud of unknowing, dedication and submission.

The last sutra above speaks about seven stages in which wisdom or prajña is cultivated. These stages may well refer to the previously mentioned various realizations in which the vrittis and the kleshas are progressively diminished. In every spiritual journey there are stages and levels; the number of divisions made depends on what aspects are found to be useful to be emphasized. According to Vyasa, the seven stages of prajña are 1) future suffering has been identified; 2) causes of suffering have been eliminated; 3) nirodha samadhi has been attained; 4) viveka has been realized; 5) the purified chitta has accomplished its purpose of providing experience and liberation; 6) any further transformation of the gunas has ceased; 7) Purusha abides in its true form. [2]

The human incarnation, which is a conjunction of Purusha and Prakriti, is for a sacred purpose. This purpose constitutes the raison d'être of a person. To search for that purpose requires a clear perception and a high level of consciousness. A development of will is necessary to be able to undertake the action which corresponds to a more awakened conscience in order to fulfill that purpose. As we understand this, we begin to see that our body—or our mind or resources or life—is not only for ourselves alone. Madame de Salzmann said, "Your body is not only yours. You need to work in order to relate the higher with the lower. That is the purpose of human existence . . . There is an energy which is trying to evolve. That is why it comes into a body. If a person works and helps the evolution of this energy, at death this energy goes to a higher level. If one does not work, the energy returns to its own level. But the human life is wasted."

Yama and Niyama

Self-restraint

2.28

योगाङ्गानुष्ठानादशुद्धिक्षये ज्ञानदीप्तिराविवेकख्यातेः

yoga-aṅga-anuṣṭhānād-aśuddhi-kṣaye jñāna-dīptir-ā-viveka-khyāteḥ

By practicing the limbs of yoga, impurity is destroyed and the radiance of jñana leads to viveka.

2.29

यमनियमासनप्राणायामप्रत्याहारधारणाध्यानसमाधयोऽष्टावङ्गानि

yama-niyama-āsana-prāṇāyāma-pratyāhāra-dhāraṇā-dhyāna-samādhayo'ṣṭāv-aṅgāni

The eight limbs of yoga are: *yama* (self-restraint), *niyama* (right observance), *asana* (right alignment or posture), *pranayama* (regulation of breath), *pratyahara* (withdrawal of the senses), *dharana* (concentration), *dhyana* (meditation), and *samadhi* (free attention).

Patañjali lists eight limbs of yoga—this is why his yoga is often given the name *ashtanga* (eight-limbed) yoga—the practice of which gradually destroys the impurities or the obstructions and leads to right discernment. Each of the eight limbs is a necessary part of the teaching of yoga. After listing the limbs, each one is elaborated further. The first five—yama, niyama, asana, pranayama, and pratyahara—together are regarded as the outer limbs of yoga, and the remaining three—dharana, dhyana, and samadhi—as internal limbs. There is not a definite linearity of progression from one limb to another, as if one limb has to be thoroughly mastered before moving on to the next limb; all the limbs can be simultaneously practiced even though there is some importance to the sequence.

It is also clear from looking at these aspects of yoga that Patañjali regards a sensitive body as necessary for spiritual realization as a clear mind and a compassionate heart.

2.30

अहिंसासत्यास्तेयब्रह्मचर्यापरिग्रहायमाः

ahiṃsā-satya-asteya-brahmacharya-aparigrahā yamāḥ

The yamas are non-violation, truthfulness, non-stealing, containment, and non-grasping.

2.31

जातिदेशकालसमयानवच्छिन्नाः सार्वभौमा महाव्रतम्

jāti-deśa-kāla-samaya-anavachchhinnāḥ sārva-bhaumā mahā-vratam

These restraints are not limited by birth, time, or circumstance; they constitute the great vow everywhere.

These yamas, and the niyamas which follow, are moral practices for the development of conscience, a gateway to higher consciousness. In many languages—for example in French, Spanish, and Sanskrit—there is only one word which covers both "consciousness" and "conscience" indicating that there is an intimate relationship between the two. As a general remark we could say that real conscience is related with higher feelings and consciousness with higher intelligence. It is a universal assertion of the sages that there can be no higher consciousness without higher conscience.

These restraints are recommended by Patañjali in all circumstances without regard to time, place or station in life. In other words, these practices are relevant across cultures, no matter what the social upbringing and material position in life.

Non-violation—Ahimsa:

The first restraint mentioned above is *ahimsa*.[3] This word is almost always translated as "non-violence." This is not wrong, but it is partial; and partiality is itself a form of *himsa*, the opposite of ahimsa. "Ahimsa" means "non-violation," "non-manipulation," and "non-interference." This certainly includes non-violence but is subtler and more comprehensive. It is necessary to distinguish between the use of violence and the use of force. It is not possible to be violent without using force, but it is possible to use force without being violent. No action can be undertaken and nothing can be accomplished without energy, power, and force. Having energy gives one power; misplaced application of energy is violence.

In the Bhagavad Gita, himsa is the violation of right order, it does not necessarily mean physical fighting or harming. For example, it is himsa by emotional blackmail if a person threatens to commit suicide unless there is an expression of love from the object of desire. External action alone does not determine whether there is himsa or not; intention, motive and the relationship between the parties involved are also relevant. Externally an action may appear violent, but it may arise because of love and compassion. "Whoever I love, I reprove and chastise" (Revelation 3:19).

In the Bhagavad Gita, Krishna urges Arjuna to fight while he maintains that the characteristics of a wise person are "ahimsa, truth, absence of anger, non-identification, peace, loyalty, compassion for all, lack of greed, gentleness, modesty, reliability" (16:2).

It is important to keep in mind a central idea of the Indian tradition, namely that of levels. There is a hierarchy of levels within a person, in the society, and in the cosmos. The lower levels in all these are lower precisely because the level of insight and understanding there is not as subtle nor as comprehensive as it is at the higher levels. For example, those parts which are at a lower level in a person or in humanity, wish to live by their own likes and dislikes and not by what is good or right for the whole person or the whole society. Those parts of us, or those among us, which understand the needs and requirements of the whole, need to persuade or educate the lower parts to obey the higher vision. Otherwise, there will be chaos internally, in the society and in the cosmos, leading to a violation (himsa) of right order (dharma) and of wholeness.

Once the idea of levels is understood, it becomes clear that the higher levels need to use force to discipline the lower levels. In order to gain an inner integration, there is an obvious place for the exercise of strength and determination in controlling the lower tendencies of the mind during the practice of yoga, or any other spiritual discipline. All transformation needs force and energy, whether this transformation is an inner one or an external (technological) one. The use of force is violent when it does not serve the purposes of the higher levels. Here are some remarks of Madame de Salzmann:

> *Make a demand upon yourself. If you don't come to something when you try, punish yourself. Deprive yourself of what you like. But have patience. Don't get angry at yourself and beat yourself. Not to try all at once, but slowly, steadily. All the time, try something. There is deep passivity. You must see this and struggle against it. If necessary, one should punish the body. Maybe one says, "Unless a connection is made, I shall not eat." Maybe one denies the body some other pleasure. The body needs to be perfectly alert and perfectly relaxed. Any tension anywhere, and the connection is broken. The body needs to be disciplined—punished or rewarded—not tortured. It must learn to obey something higher. The body needs to be available.*

Ahimsa needs to be understood not in terms of appearances and external forms of conduct, but in relation to the internal intention and order involved. Egotistic intent and motivation, however placid, peaceful, and non-harming the external behavior may be, always carry seeds of violence in their very core. Krishnamurti said, "As long as I am, love is not." As long as the ego is in charge, which is to say as long as there is selfishness, all our actions are without love. If we act without love, there is a violation of the spirit. Ahimsa in full measure is not possible for a person as long as the person is ego-centered. There are many relative levels of freedom from violence and manipulation. Ahimsa is not accomplished once forever, and we need to continually search for its dynamic source. Only at the highest level of being can someone naturally manifest ahimsa; below that we can only approach it.

True ahimsa is a property of the real world where it is a natural consequence of insight, as are compassion and love. To fix its understanding as non-harming at the level of the ordinary world is like taking sentimental love and attachment as the core of the compassion of the Buddha or of Christ. Giving an exclusive importance to avoiding physical harm, and not taking into account the mental, psychological, and spiritual anguish caused by our actions, further strengthens the fallacy that a person is primarily a body, a fallacy which all spiritual traditions are at pains to dispel.

Only a sage on the mountaintop of consciousness sees the proper place of everything and everyone; such a person comes to a deep-seated acceptance of all there is. But all the sages who return to the world in order to be active in it and to teach others, commend struggle—always internal and sometimes external. Perhaps it is only by an endless struggle between the higher energies of consciousness and the lower ones of forgetfulness that the play of forces, which constitute the cosmos, continues. A complete destruction of one side or the other would bring this play to a halt—a possibility only for the end of days when time shall be no more. Otherwise, as Krishna says in *The Mahabharata*, the choice is not between battle (*yuddha*) and absence of it, but only between one kind of battle or another. The real question then concerns the level of the battle we are going to fight. As St. Paul says, "Finally then, find your strength in the Lord, in His mighty power . . . For our fight is not against human foes, but against cosmic powers, against the authorities and potentates of this dark world, against the superhuman forces of evil in the heavens" (Ephesians 6:10-12).

Truthfulness—Satya:

The next restraint is satya which means truth, truthfulness, sincerity, authenticity. Satya is closely associated with rita which was spoken about earlier (see 1.48-49). Though in its original intrinsic sense, rita transcends the power of space and time, the gods apply it to the affairs of the universe in the form of satya. Also, it is said that rita and satya were born from tapas, self-discipline (Rig Veda X.190.1), and are thus twins—coexistent and coeternal. In this connection, it is useful to recall sutra 2.1 in which tapas is said to be one of the three fundamental practices of yoga.

Just as the practice of ahimsa, the practice of telling the truth, or of not lying, has many levels. When we speak of what we do not know, when we are partial, and when we are convinced that we know all there is to know about something, we lie. We lie when we speak as if we are the center of the universe and can pass judgment on everyone and everything. We lie when we weave fantasies in our minds and do not see the way it is. All theological arguments—about whether Christ is ultimately of the same substance as God or not, or whether the Divine Nature is that of trinity or unity, or whether Atman is identically the same as Brahman or different—cannot not be lies. Those who know about God or Brahman, such as the Christ or the Buddha or Ramana Maharishi, do not engage in arguments. They say what they see, not what they have read or heard or thought. The gospel writer says of Christ that "he spoke as one with authority, not as the scribes do" (Mark 1:22). Christ himself warned his disciples: "Beware of the scribes [in order to make the context more relevant to our situation, we should not hesitate in substituting here "theologians," "scholars," "priests," and "pundits" and the like] who like to walk about in long robes, and who love salutations in the market-places, and first seats in the synagogues, and first places at suppers; who devour the houses of widows, and as a pretext make long prayers. These shall receive a harsher judgment" (Luke 20:46-47).

The grand enunciations of the sages and the scriptures which are beyond our experience can invite us to wonder and inquire and to undertake the sadhana which can lead us to see what the sages saw. We are not equally drawn to all great utterances, but it is wise to refrain from theological disputes. The first requirement of self-knowledge is sincerity and as we begin to see the various ways we lie, we can understand the need for practicing truthfulness.

Non-stealing—Asteya:

Non-stealing (*asteya*) is not only refraining from taking something that does not belong to us, but also taking or accepting some privileges without making a proper payment for them. This is especially important in the vertical dimension of spiritual hierarchy. To acquire some insight from the sages or from the tradition, or to assume some advantages from the society or the family, without paying something back with a corresponding responsibility is theft. According to the Shatapatha Brahmana (I.7.2: 1-5), when a person is born, simultaneously obligations or debts to the gods, to the sages, to the ancestors, and to the community are born. If we do not attempt to pay these debts by appropriate forms of payment—for example, by studying the teachings of the sages and trying to live them—we continue to be selfish thieves. Krishna says in the Bhagavad Gita: "Foster the gods with *yajña* (sacrifice, sacred exchange of energy between levels) as they foster you; by nourishing each other, you will attain the supreme good. Fostered by yajña, the gods will bestow on you the joys you cherish. Those who enjoy the gift of the gods without giving to them in return are verily thieves" (3:10-12).

Containment—Brahmacharya:

Brahmacharya is almost always translated as sexual chastity or continence, but it literally means "dwelling in Brahman." Brahman literally means the Vastness. To dwell in the Vastness, which is possible only when one is freed of self-occupation and me-me-me, is the real brahmacharya. However, everywhere there is special fixation and fascination with sex. Whenever people are asked about sin, they think first of all of sex, but the first sin in any category of sins, as listed in any tradition, is "pride" or "self-importance." In any case, we need not underestimate the force and importance of sex. The whole of nature is driven by this energy. Even the Buddha is said to have said that if there were another force as strong as sex, he would not have realized enlightenment. Gurdjieff said in one of his talks: "Seventy-five percent of thought and feeling comes from sex."

In many spiritual teachings, much emphasis is placed on sexual abstinence, with the understanding that the sexual energy can be transmuted into spiritual energy. That is true, but what is most important to note is that this transmutation is possible only when an intense spiritual effort (*tapas*) is undertaken; otherwise, if abstinence is adhered to as a religious injunction, without the accompanying effort of awareness, of meditation or of prayer and other forms of spiritual practice, the mind is likely to dwell on various sexual pleasures in fantasy. As a result, more harm is done to the pursuit of the purification of the mind by this than by engaging in sexual acts. Quite often, feelings of guilt and an accompanying anxiety about punishment result from an occupation with sex. This may lead to vehement attempts to cover up the inner states of the mind or to fanatic reactions against those who are suspected of indulging in sexual pleasures.

When Madame de Salzmann was asked about the need for sexual continence during intensive periods of the practice of the work, she said, "The work takes a lot of sexual energy. When it is needed, it will be taken. Sex energy can be used in the work, but only when one is very advanced. At present don't do anything about it, otherwise, one can do something wrong. It is like food and drink. The body needs it and wants it; it is quite right."

It is the experience of many serious students of yoga that an intensive practice of yoga uses up a lot of sexual energy, leaving the sadhaka without much interest in sexual activity. But the reverse is also true on occasion. There are situations when an intensive spiritual practice is accompanied by an enhanced sexual energy. On one occasion of sustained work, Madame de Salzmann was asked about the relationship of sex with subtler and higher energy experienced during practice. She said, "This energy touches every part of the body, including sex. Then one feels the sexual impulse and wants to express it. But one does not always have to have the usual action."

Attachment to sexual pleasures is one of the major supports of ego, and its addiction to self-occupation. The important thing is to return to the real meaning of brahmacharya, to dwell in Brahman, the Vastness. All practice of yoga is intended to assist us in relating us more and more with the subtler and vaster realities, in which we live and move and have our true being. In this effort, a repeated practice of containment of all our energies—of sex, of mind, of speech as well as of feeling—is required, always searching for the right balance between indulgence and deprivation.

Non-grasping—Aparigraha:

Non-possession or non-grasping (*aparigraha*) is recommended as a practice by Patañjali. It is as relevant to psychological possessions as to the physical or material ones. The force of possession is primarily psychological and we can be addicted to an accumulation of goods, of power, of knowledge, or of thrilling experiences. That is why there is the repeated suggestion by the sages, such as Krishnamurti, that in order to be free, one needs to die to the habit of accumulation. Dying to oneself is to die to this accumulator, which is more psychological than physical.

We can, as can a whole culture, become addicted to acquiring more and more possessions. Among the temptations which Mara tried in order to waylay the great yogi Siddhartha, the Buddha-to-be, was possession. Mara offered to turn a nearby mountain into a mountain of gold if Siddhartha would abandon his search for Truth. But, owing to a clear abhyasa of steady viveka, Siddhartha was able to persist in vairagya towards all temptations in the realm of Prakriti. It is said that as Siddhartha understood that Mara was a part of himself, a projection of his own mind, he became the Buddha, realizing his identity with nothing less than Purusha, free of all the projections of Prakriti, either alluring or frightening.

The social forces of advertising are geared to manipulate our sense of greed and fear, in creating competition with others for more and more possessions. It is important to understand the force of possessiveness, acquisitiveness, and grasping in ourselves as well as in our culture. Ironically, it is our inborn wish for a greater being that ignorance turns into a wish, or even a need, for more and more possessions. Unless we see the strength of acquisitiveness in ourselves—for wealth, fame, information, knowledge, experience and approval of others—we will not appreciate the need to struggle against this tendency to rid our psyche of this obstacle.

Observances

2.32

शौचसंतोषतपः स्वाध्यायेश्वरप्रणिधानानि नियमाः

śaucha-saṃtoṣa-tapaḥ-svādhyāya-īśvara-praṇidhānāni niyamāḥ

The niyamas are purity, contentment, self-discipline (*tapas*), self-study (*svadhyaya*), and dedication to Ishvara.

2.33

वितर्कबाधने प्रतिपक्षभावनम्

vitarka-bādhane pratipakṣa-bhāvanam

When negative thoughts and feelings arise, the opposite should be cultivated.

2.34

वितर्का हिंसादयः कृतकारितानुमोदिता लोभक्रोधमोहपूर्वका मृदुमध्याधिमात्रा दुःखाज्ञानानन्तफला इति प्रतिपक्षभावनम्

vitarkā hiṃsā-ādayaḥ kṛta-kārita-anumoditā lobha-krodha-moha-pūrvakā mṛdu-madhya-adhimātrā duḥkha-ajñāna-ananta-phalā iti pratipakṣa-bhāvanam

Cultivating the opposite is realizing that negative feelings, such as that of violence, result in endless suffering and ignorance—whether these feelings are acted out, instigated or condoned, whether motivated by greed, anger, or delusion, whether these are mild, medium, or extreme.

Three of the niyamas (observances)—tapas, svadhyaya, and Ishvara pranidhana—were included in the practices of kriya yoga, in sutra 2.1. As was mentioned earlier, while commenting on that sutra, these three practices—self-discipline, self-study, and dedication to God—are intimately connected with each other; one is not possible without the other.

Cleanliness or purity—of the heart and of the mind more than of the body—is clearly an important aim and practice. What we feel in our heart is closer to the spirit than what we do with our body. It is much more important to have freedom from anger and hatred in our heart than to be free of dirt. The great saint and poet Kabir says:

> *Ages have passed turning the beads,*
> *But turning the heart has not occurred.*
> *Put aside the beads of the hand,*
> *And turn the beads of the heart.*[4]

It is possible to get too occupied with external purity. Some Brahmins can get upset if even the shadow of a *shudra*, a person of the lowest caste, falls on them. In my own experience, I was saddened to discover that a Sanskrit teacher in Varanasi felt obliged to go and bathe in the sacred river Ganga in order to purify himself after giving me a lesson. I was considered impure because I had started learning Sanskrit in a foreign country and from a woman. As Vivekananda so strongly and with much sorrow expressed, some Brahmins have forgotten the need of the purification of the heart and have turned Hinduism into "Don't Touchism."

Contentment rarely enters the list of virtues in the scheme of Western philosophers. They often include courage, truth, bravery, humility, but not contentment. It is important, of course, that contentment does not become a heedless acceptance of the status quo which is fostered by laziness and strengthens the force of abhinivesha. The value of the practice of contentment lies in its effect in freeing us from hankering after more and more. Especially in the matter of external possessions and physical comforts, contentment with what we have can free us to turn attention to concerns which are more essential for the welfare of our soul.

Even though the aim of yoga is to go beyond what we ordinarily term good or bad, and to be free of all personal thoughts and feelings so that we could be established in the suprapersonal intelligence beyond thought, when we are invaded by negative thoughts and emotions which pervert the practice of yama and niyama, it is useful to cultivate the opposite feelings and ideas. For example, if a feeling of unfriendliness or hatred arises towards someone, we need to search for something about that person which we can admire and be grateful for.

Whatever be the cause of these negative feelings and thoughts, and whatever their intensity, and whether these feelings are externally acted out or not, they affect us. No amount of self-justification in having bad feelings is useful. It is for the sake of our own physical, psychological and spiritual well being that we need to be free of negative thoughts and feelings, as well as for the sake of the others and of the world. An increasing recognition and understanding that negative attitudes, such as of violence or jealousy or greed, cause suffering and increase ignorance, both for ourselves and as well as for others, help us to see that they need to be overcome. Also, any effort of not giving into the negative feelings increasingly reveals to us both their strength and the immense amount of harm done by them. The practice of cultivating the opposite feelings acts as a counter current to minimize the negative feelings.

▪ Being Established in Yama and Niyama

2.35

अहिंसाप्रतिष्ठायां तत्संनिधौ वैरत्यागः

ahiṃsā-pratiṣṭhāyāṃ tat-saṃnidhau vaira-tyāgaḥ

In the presence of one who is established in ahimsa, there is cessation of hostility.

2.36

सत्यप्रतिष्ठायां क्रियाफलाश्रयत्वम्

satya-pratiṣṭhāyām kriyā-phala-āśrayatvam

When one abides in truthfulness, actions result in their desired end.

2.37

अस्तेयप्रतिष्ठायां सर्वरत्नोपस्थानम्

asteya-pratiṣṭhāyāṃ sarva-ratna-upasthānam

When one is established in non-stealing, riches present themselves freely.

The practice of yama and niyama leads to many benedictions. As was mentioned earlier, ahimsa is not only non-harming physically, it is non-violation, and therefore lack of manipulation, as well as non-imposition. It is important to emphasize that in the presence of someone who is established in ahimsa, hostility or enmity is abandoned, not only by human beings but even by animals. It is a part of the traditional folklore that cobras or lions or other animals are not violent in the presence of a person established in ahimsa. There are stories about many saints—especially about the Buddha and the Christ—in whose presence both the lamb and the lion could be together without fear or hostility.

The fundamental principle of true ecology is ahimsa, non-violation and non-manipulation. All action arising from an idea of doing good leads to manipulation and violence. From true insight right action follows automatically, without deciding to do the right action. Usually when we decide to do the right thing, thinking enters and mental ideals occupy our attention. Besides, expectations are set up both about ourselves as well as about the recipients of our good deeds, preparing the ground for disappointment and resentment.

Laura Huxley, the wife of the well-known writer Aldous Huxley reported an incident with Krishnamurti. On one occasion in a small gathering, he was saying that one should not go about doing good. She reminded him that he goes around the world doing good. "Not intentionally," he said. The point is that a rose does not decide to smell like a rose; it is from the fragrance that we conclude that it is a rose. Similarly, a sage does not decide to do good or to be compassionate; these attitudes are a natural by-product of their wisdom. To say that the Buddha is wise but not compassionate is an oxymoron.

Great sages do not practice virtue or compassion or good works; these kinds of behavior are a natural outcome of their quality of being. When established in the yamas and niyamas, a person's atmosphere changes. In other modes of speaking, the aura of the person changes or the subtle vibrations emanating from the person change in quality, influencing all those who come in their presence. The good do good by merely being good.

The middle path, which is not a middling path, requires that we not decide things once and for all. We need to be awake to the situation and the right response will follow. That is the practice of yoga. This is why the path is said in the Katha Upanishad to be as sharp as a razor's edge. Krishnamurti said, "Be totally attentive and do nothing." The needful and the true action will flower from the soil of choiceless insight.

There is a strong tendency in all of us which makes us ask for clear rules and regulations which can be decided before-hand and can be applied in all circumstances. This tendency is further enhanced in the name of dharma, which means law, order, duty, responsibility. But yoga requires a vigilance and an awareness arising from being present here and now, to this situation, at this time and responding to it. Dharma has to do with doing the right thing; yoga has to do with being the right person. Dharma leads towards making a system, yoga requires being present. Thus there is always a tension between dharma and yoga. By having definite rules and regulations, we can become bureaucrats of consciousness; but if someone is in charge—if we are present—then the rules can be suspended in a particular case, or applied differently. Being awake to the situation, we will be able to see what is needed and act accordingly.

Abiding in truthfulness gives a great deal of force. There are many stories in India in which a person invokes a life-long adherence to truthfulness and asks for the protection of higher forces in overcoming the laws of physical nature at the ordinary level. Such a person cannot be burnt by fire or drowned by water, much to the amazement of everyone. Actions of such truthful people result in their desired end, however strong the odds against them.

Even though the sutra (2.37) above literally speaks in terms of jewels flying to one established in non-stealing, it is not to be taken so materialistically. What is suggested is that whatever is needed by those established in non-stealing comes to them quite unexpectedly. The first requirement of non-stealing is gratitude and a recognition of what one has been given. Those who have gratitude come to realize that whatever they have is precious.

2.38

ब्रह्मचर्यप्रतिष्ठायां वीर्यलाभः

brahmacharya-pratiṣṭhāyām vīrya-lābhaḥ

When brahmacharya is established, great vigor is obtained.

2.39

अपरिग्रहस्थैर्ये जन्मकथंतासंबोधः

aparigraha-sthairye janma-kathaṃtā-saṃbodhaḥ

When one is established in non-grasping, there is knowledge of the nature and purpose of existence.

2.40

शौचात्स्वाङ्गजुगुप्सा परैरसंसर्गः

śauchāt-svā-aṅga-jugupsā parair-asaṃsargaḥ

Purity leads to non-identification with one's own body and to a freedom from the need for contact with others.

2.41

सत्त्वशुद्धिसौमनस्यैकाग्र्येन्द्रियजयात्मदर्शनयोग्यत्वानि च

sattva-śuddhi-saumanasya-eka-agrya-indriya-jaya-ātma-darśana-yogyatvāni cha

Purity of mind, cheerfulness, mastery of the senses, one-pointedness, and ability for Self-realization follow.

2.42

संतोषादनुत्तमः सुखलाभः

saṃtoṣād-anuttamaḥ sukha-lābhaḥ

Contentment leads to unsurpassed joy.

2.43

कायेन्द्रियसिद्धिरशुद्धिक्षयात्तपसः

kāya-indriya-siddhir-aśuddhi-kṣayāt-tapasaḥ

Self-discipline leads to the destruction of impurity and to the perfection of the body and the senses.

2.44

स्वाध्यायादिष्टदेवतासंप्रयोगः

svādhyāyād-iṣṭa-devatā-saṃprayogaḥ

From self-study one reaches union with the chosen deity (*ishta devata*).

2.45

समाधिसिद्धिरीश्वरप्रणिधानात्

samādhi-siddhir-īśvara-praṇidhānāt

Perfection in samadhi arises from dedication to Ishvara.

Brahmacharya was spoken about above in connection with general comments on all the yamas. Some comments were also made about non-acquisitiveness (aparigraha). As is clearly emphasized in sutra 2.39 above, aparigraha needs to be understood much more widely than as the non-acquisition of material goods. There can be a grasping for knowledge or for experiences or fame. Freedom from acquisitiveness in the widest sense will bring about an understanding of the nature and purpose of existence. Greed has a tendency to squeeze the whole vastness into the smallness of me-me-me. Freedom from acquisitiveness allows us to accept our situation and the world as it is and to be related with the whole more and more joyously.

Sutra 2.40 is a reminder of what all the great traditions have asserted: the person is not the body; therefore the death of the body is not the death of the person. Developed yogis naturally become more and more aware of the fact that they are not their bodies. However, we should be aware that this sutra has sometimes been interpreted to mean that a yogi should develop disgust for the body. Following this notion, all sorts of rules and prohibitions get formulated, such as a yogi cannot be in the physical presence of a woman. We find a similar sort of extremism on Mount Athos, the holy mountain for Orthodox Christians: this mountain is dedicated to the Virgin Mary, and there can be no other female presence, even among the animals. However Patañjali emphasizes a purity of mind, as is clear from the very next sutra.

It is always easier to get stuck on surface understandings rather than to search for the deeper meaning. Literal interpretations of scriptures or the teachings of the sages result from understanding spiritual realities materially. There is an incident described in the life of the famous sixteenth-century saint, Mira. She was a great devotee of Krishna, wedded to him in her heart and soul. Once a well-known yogi came and stayed for a short while at the edge of the town where Mira lived. Mira wished to meet this great yogi and sent word to that effect. Her request was refused because the yogi said that his spiritual practice forbade any contact with a female. Mira, who understood the need for all aspirants to be deeply receptive to the Divine active initiative, sent a word to him saying,

"O Yogi, I should have thought that in the presence of Krishna we are all females."

It is said that the famous yogi was pierced to the core of his being by the spear of insight, and came running to Mira and adopted her as his teacher.

It is necessary to be satisfied with what we have, to be contented with our situation if we are going to be dedicated to and have enough energy for a serious search of subtler realities. Otherwise, there is no end to our wanting. In the process of an impartial self-study, it is important to ask ourselves: "What or how much is enough?" "What is needed for me to be able to turn towards what really matters?"

Āsana, Prāṇāyāma, and Pratyāhāra

Right Alignment

2.46

स्थिरसुखमासनम्

sthira-sukham-āsanam

Right alignment (*asana*) is accompanied by steadiness and ease.

2.47

प्रयत्नशैथिल्यानन्तसमापत्तिभ्याम्

prayatna-śaithilya -ananta-samāpattibhyām

This is attained when there is complete relaxation and samapatti (fusion, union) with the Infinite.

2.48

ततो द्वन्द्वानभिघातः

tato dvandva-anabhighātaḥ

Then one is no longer assailed by opposing dualities.

It is clear from these three sutras that Patañjali places a great deal of emphasis on right posture or alignment and that alignment or posture is not to be taken only in a physical sense. We see a similar emphasis in the Zen tradition, especially in Soto Zen. Dogen Zenzi said, "Zen is nothing but zazen, sitting rightly." The search for right alignment is the effort to align the personal self with the Infinite so that there is the right flow of energies inside, from above downwards. Although asanas refer to physical posture, the emotional and the mental postures are also important in the search for right alignment. The word for "posture" is in French "*attitude*"—a reminder of the inclusion of the inner state as well as the outer position in the right posture.

Madame de Salzmann so much emphasized the right bodily posture as a prerequisite for a higher quality of attention. At one moment, sitting very straight in her chair, she said that body posture is all. "If the ankle or the arm is one way rather than another, the connection is lost, and the higher energy cannot pass. If even a foot is not rightly aligned, the connection with the higher energy can be broken . . . Higher enregy is there but cannot come down unless the body is available and in equilibrium, without tension. Everyone is imprisoned in their physical postures and attitudes, and the consequent emotional and mental postures. It is necessary to find a way of being which frees one from this limitation. It is necessary to find a connection with higher energy."

The relationship between effort and grace, between a path and pathlessness, between discipline and freedom requires an ongoing search. All transformation and insight come from levels above ourselves, but a preparation of the psychosomatic organism can make us more available and receptive to what comes from above. Nirvana is uncaused freedom and no effort can bring it about in any determined manner. However, the eightfold path is highly recommended to all searchers who wish to reach Nirvana. Each one of us needs to discover the proper balance between the masculine and feminine energies, between the active and the receptive. We find a classical image and expressions of this in *Ardhanaranarishvara* (half male half female) forms of Shiva, the Lord of Yoga. The image of woman above and man below where the woman faces upwards and man downwards in some Tantric paintings conveys the need to be receptive to the higher and to be active with respect to the world for which we are responsible. Meister Eckhart said, "What we receive in contemplation, we give out in love."

No particular yoga posture is mentioned by Patañjali. Initially one has to struggle to find the right posture so that the body is more and more rightly aligned to permit the harmonious flow of energies inside. Much vigilance is needed to guard the inner temple so that the marauding forces of stray thoughts do not invade the sanctuary, causing a deviation from the true inner form and outer posture. Finding and maintaining the right posture needs an active and alert attention. On the other hand, the right alignment aids the maintenance of an active attention.

Soon the need to act as a warrior gives way to the possibility of becoming a lover who is naturally interested in the connection with the subtler energies. When there is a right alignment with the Infinite, it is possible to let go of all effort, all struggle, and all tension. Then even the image of a lover is no longer relevant; the searcher is now like the beloved who is embraced by the lover who was earlier longed for. In this union, there is no longer any struggle between opposites, between above and below, between lover and beloved. Not only is there a physical relaxation, but also an emotional and mental reconciliation of dualities.

The Breath of Life

2.49

तस्मिन्सति श्वासप्रश्वासयोर्गतिविच्छेदः प्राणायामः

tasmin-sati śvāsa-praśvāsayor-gati-vichchhedaḥ prāṇāyāmaḥ

With right alignment, the regulation of the flow of breath in and out is pranayama.

2.50

बाह्याभ्यन्तरस्तम्भवृत्तिर्देशकालसंख्याभिः परिदृष्टो दीर्घसूक्ष्मः

bāhya-abhyantara-stambha-vṛttir-deśa-kāla-saṃkhyābhiḥ paridṛṣṭo dīrgha-sūkṣmaḥ

When the movement of breath in and out and the stopping of breath are observed, according to time, place, and number, breathing becomes deep and subtle.

2.51

बाह्याभ्यन्तरविषयाक्षेपी चतुर्थः

bāhya-abhyantara-viṣaya-ākṣepī chaturthaḥ

The fourth stage of pranayama takes one beyond the domain of inner and outer.

Patañjali has emphasized the importance of right breathing in controlling the distractions of the mind (see sutra 1.34, and the comments on it which follow). Here more emphasis is placed on this important subject. It is worth remarking again that prana is not simply breath in the ordinary sense of the word. It refers to the whole spectrum of vital energies, much like Chi (or Qi) in the Chinese spiritual traditions. Ordinary breath is the least subtle aspect of prana which also includes all levels of subtle life energies. After finding the right posture and alignment, if we simply watch our breath, the quality of breathing changes. Yoga masters have developed many techniques of varying the length of inhalation, exhalation, and the retention of breath inside or outside. When the breath is focused on different parts of the body, those parts are energized with the subtler and subtler components of prana, producing subtle sensations inside. We have a privileged position with respect to the processes which take place within our body and we can become aware of the subtle changes which take place inside.

The fourth stage of pranayama is not elaborated by Patañjali. It may refer to the sort of extremely slow breathing attested to in the Yoga literature which refers to the fact that a yogi can be in a closed space without any perceptible breathing activity for a long time. This is clearly a very advanced stage of psychic and physical development, requiring a long and steady work. Practice of these advanced kinds of breathing exercises is not recommended until the searcher has purified the body, mind and emotions by a serious engagement with yoga.

At any stage of practice of pranayama there is an expansion of the inside to include what is usually outside, and an obliteration of the boundary between the internal and external domains of existence. It is as if the psyche and the cosmos become interpenetrated; then because of their isomorphism, by studying oneself internally one can acquire knowledge of the cosmos. Psychology and cosmology thus become one seamless science. This is the basis of many sutras in the third chapter of the *Yoga Sutras*.

2.52

ततः क्षीयते प्रकाशावरणम्

tataḥ kṣīyate prakāśa-āvaraṇam

Then the covering over the inner light of truth is dissolved.

2.53

धारणासु च योग्यता मनसः

dhāraṇāsu cha yogyatā manasaḥ

And the mind (*manas*) becomes fit for dharana.

The whole of yoga practice is an aid to the removal of the veil covering the face of Truth. The veil is that of our sleepiness, the quite lawful tendencies of our lower nature. The sutra (2.52) above is very reminiscent of the Isha Upanishad where the sole seer, Purusha, is Pushan, the Sun: "The face of Truth is covered with a golden disk. Unveil it, O Pushan, so that I who love the Truth may see it" (verse 15). A yogi is naturally a lover of Truth, and when the veil is dissolved, the mind gradually becomes fit for the first stages of meditation, dharana—concentration.

Withdrawal of the Senses

2.54

स्वविषयासंप्रयोगे चित्तस्य स्वरूपानुकार इवेन्द्रियाणां प्रत्याहारः

sva-viṣaya-asaṃprayoge chittasya sva-rūpa-anukāra iva-indriyāṇāṃ pratyāhāraḥ

Pratyahara is the withdrawal of the senses from their objects by following the essential nature of the mind.

2.55

ततः परमा वश्यतेन्द्रियाणाम्

tataḥ paramā vaśyata-indriyāṇām

From this comes the perfect mastery over the senses.

Quieting of chitta is aided by the reduction in sensory stimulation. We can withdraw from an attachment to, or even attention to, external objects anywhere, even in a market place. However this process is helped by having fewer external stimuli because we tend to be seduced by the external. This is why in so many monasteries, or meditation halls, dark colors rather than the bright ones are used. We need to practice an inward attention by turning from looking outward to an inward perception. The inward extension of the senses is analogous to outward seeing, hearing, touching, tasting, and smelling, but inward perception has different possibilities. There is a vast inner world and as we become more and more sensitive inward, we can begin to be aware of deeper and deeper aspects of ourselves.

Cutting out the external stimuli does not by itself reduce the vrittis of the mind; in fact, fear or imagination can enter and agitate the mind. Depending on their psychic make up, for some people, closing the eyes or being quiet produces anxiety and increases mental agitation. In such situations it is better to undertake the practice of yoga—whether physical yoga or meditation—with other people with whom one is comfortable and at ease. Gradually, as we see more and more clearly their roots, the fears and the imaginings will diminish. Mental distractions are harder to overcome when practicing alone. It is said on Mount Athos, the holy mountain of Eastern Orthodox Christianity, that a solitary monk is much more tempted by the Devil than the monks in a community.

It is commonly understood that a wandering mind, drawn to this sense-object or that sensual experience, is the problem. Therefore there is sometimes a wish to bypass the mind—more like blowing the mind—with excessive drugs, alcohol, loud music, sex, strobe lights, excessive stimulation. But at what cost? The use of powerful mind affecting drugs depletes subtle alchemical substances which aid the power of attention. This may lead to a more subtle kind of attention deficit disorder than is usually recognized. The procedure followed in pratyahara is just the reverse: here the senses are withdrawn from the objects as the mind gradually turns inward in meditation. In this process, the mind is not destroyed, but the energies which are continually turned outward are harnessed so that attention can be given to subtler and deeper levels inside. A subtler attention is called for and developed in this process.

It is unfortunate that even in some of the sayings of the great sages and sacred texts, we come across expressions indicating the need to destroy the mind rather than to transcend it and to harness its energies. For example, Ramana Maharishi often speaks of the necessity of *manonash*; this literally means the "destruction of the mind." And we find Madame Blavatsky saying in *The Voice of the Silence*, "Mind is the slayer of truth, slay the slayer." It is certainly true that the mind is always introducing its own subjectivity and distractions, thus covering the truth with fantasy, but if the metaphorical language is taken literally, the mind would not be able to play its necessary role. Patañjali is much more interested in the purification of the mind so that it can become a proper instrument of true perception.

It should also be noted that silence is not absence of sound. We can easily test this in wilderness which can be full of sound, but if we feel the presence of the peace and the vastness and we can let go of our inner talk, we feel a silence. Some sounds, usually natural and coherent ones, can enhance the sense of silence. A sense of wonder brings silence because we are silenced. The aim of good music is to lead to an inner silence, through the call to listen without commentary. An inner silence brings us a different experience of being as it connects us to the subtler vibrations within ourselves and outside ourselves. If we do not have the experience of an inner silence, and if suddenly everyone around us becomes silent, we can become apprehensive, usually because we imagine we are the center of the universe, and that others are talking about us or shutting us out by their silence. Consequently, in the culture at large, more inclined to commerce than to the cultivation of inner silence, almost everywhere we find some background music or noise.

Just as silence is not absence of sound, stillness is not absence of motion, as one can see in the performance of an exquisite *Bharat Natyam* dance, or in the sculptures of the dancing Shiva, where the movement highlights, protects, and enhances stillness. We have the experience of stillness in action, when we know what is needed and we are able to carry it out without an inner agitation. In such situations, we can begin to understand the call and the possibility of an inner connection. "Be still, and know that I AM" (Psalm 46:10). "The Lord will fight for you; you need only be still"(Exodus 14:14).

We can be much aided by an external silence and a physical stillness; these affect the mind and help in bringing about internal quiet. Both silence and stillness are characteristics of presence, of being present, of being here and now, where there is no time. This is why those who are deeply innerly quiet can be engaged in any activity and be in meditation; they do not have to sit down or adopt any particular posture for meditation. If we could be completely centered and still, the right action would be done through us. Everything comes to those who do not crave for anything.

Endnotes:

1 In this context, please see R. Ravindra, *The Gospel of John in the Light of Indian Mysticism*; especially chapters 6 and 14.

2 Adapted from the quote from Vyasa provided by Christopher Chapple and Yogi Ananda Viraj, p. 68.

3 The readers' attention is drawn to an article "Ahimsa, Transformation and Ecology" in *The Spiritual Roots of Yoga*.

4 In the Hindi original, the lines are very simple and beautiful and employ a charming play on the word *manaka*, which means both "bead" and "of the heart (mind)." In the original, the lines are:

Manaka pherata yuga bhaya,
Bhaya na manaka phera.
Karaka manaka chhandike,
Manaka manaka phera.

Vibhuti-Pada

▪

The Way of Splendor

Discipline and Transformations

Total Attention

3.1

देशबन्धश्चित्तस्य धारणा

deśa-bandhaś-chittasya dhāraṇā

Dharana is holding the mind in one place.

3.2

तत्र प्रत्ययैकतानता ध्यानम्

tatra pratyaya-ekatānatā dhyānam

Dhyana is the uninterrupted flow of awareness towards the object of attention.

3.3

तदेवार्थमात्रनिर्भासं स्वरूपशून्यमिव समाधिः

tad-eva-artha-mātra-nirbhāsaṃ sva-rūpa-śūnyam-iva samādhiḥ

Samadhi is the state when the self is not, when there is awareness only of the object of meditation.

After enumerating the five external limbs of yoga—yama, niyama, asana, pranayama, and pratyahara—in the previous chapter, Patañjali elaborates the three inner limbs—dharana, dhyana, and samadhi. These three inner limbs are all different kinds of attention. The last of the external limbs and the first two of the internal limbs, namely pratyahara, dharana, and dhyana, constitute one continuous process of interiorization.

Dharana, concentration, is the warrior or masculine phase of sadhana. As Madame de Salzmann repeatedly advised, "Stay in front." Struggle, determination, will and effort are all relevant and applicable in the process of dharana. It is like bringing a flashlight into a dark room and pointing to one particular object in order to bring it into focus.

Dhyana, usually translated as "meditation," is more like a general illumination in a room rather than a flashlight focused on one object.[1] It involves knowing the relationships between the parts and the whole, and the relationship of one thing with respect to another. This kind of attention is closer to being available and surrendering to something subtler. It requires a receptivity to finer energies. It is the lover or feminine phase of sadhana.

Samadhi is a state in which the "I" does not exist as separate from the object of attention. It is a state of self-naughting, the state spoken of in Buddhism as *akinchan*, a state of freedom from myself or a freedom from egoism. There is no observer separate from the observed, no subject separate from the object. Only the knowledge gained in such states of consciousness can be called objective in the true sense of the word; otherwise, it is more or less subjective. Even scientific knowledge which has been considered to be objective because it is intersubjective, amenable to verification by competent researchers everywhere, is not objective in the sense of being completely free of subjectivity.

It is useful to remark that there is nothing wrong with the existence of the ego. Without a strong ego, there would be no possibility of the warrior stage of dharana. However, the difficulty arises when the ego takes over and assumes that it constitutes the whole of myself, with its attendant self-importance. Here are some remarks of Madame de Salzmann directly relevant to the question of the ego:

> *The important thing is to be. If there is no real I, then the ego takes over. Energy cannot be without relationship. If it does not serve I intentionally, then it automatically serves the ego. Watch for the point in working when it is necessary to let go. Something has to be abandoned. Ego makes the*

> *effort, but one comes to a point when the ego has to be passive. The point of transition is subtle. There can be too much effort or too little. Unless there is the I, there is only the ego. So let it be. One recognizes the presence of I from the fact that I wishes to serve. Ego does not wish to serve. But until there is the I, let the ego be. It can be useful. What else are you going to do? When the I appears, the ego automatically loses energy and becomes unimportant. It can still be there but it is not in control. When real individuality is there, the ego finds its proper place. For some people, Mr. Gurdjieff used to advise them to develop their ego because they were too weak. Then later, when it is not needed to be the master, he would ask them to soak it in cold water.*

It is important for sadhakas to keep their attention oriented towards the radiant flower of wisdom, Purusha, the real I, rather than getting too immersed in the weeds of the ego which are always there. With self-study, we see and acknowledge the mischievous maneuverings of our ego, but again and again we need to return to what is of real interest—the real Self. As a Chinese classic puts it, "When the lion is departed from the mountain, the monkey becomes the king." When the real I is not present to us, we are ruled by the monkey ego.

This is a fundamental point in Indian thought and needs to be emphasized. The whole tradition is unanimous in insisting that deep down, at the very core of ourselves, we are divine. One of the four great utterances (*mahavakyas*) of the Hindu tradition is "I am Brahman."[2] We do not live in actuality from the truth of this identity—which itself is real as far as all the sages in India are concerned. The purpose of spiritual practice is to actualize the real. If we get thoroughly immersed in the actual—the state of sleep, or of mechanicality, or of illusion, or of sinfulness, depending on the tradition from which we approach this—we can get disheartened and feel guilt-ridden. Such attitudes can lead to weakness, but inner strength, and feelings of courage and hope are needed to undertake the arduous task of transformation. Spiritual teachings are teachings of hope. Sages may describe our actual situation in stark terms, emphasizing the terror of our human situation, but they always point to a level of reality free from suffering, illusion and sin, and assure us that it is possible to connect with what is real, however difficult the journey.

The great nineteenth-century Indian saint, Ramakrishna, told a story about a tigress who attacked a herd of goats. Shot by a hunter just as she sprang on her prey, the tigress gave birth to a cub and died. The cub grew up in the company of the goats. Following their example, it started eating grass and bleating like them, even when it grew to be a big tiger. One day another tiger attacked the flock and was amazed to see a grass eating tiger in the flock. When the wild tiger caught up to the grass eating tiger, the latter began to bleat. The wild tiger dragged the other to the water and asked it to look at its face in the water and see that it was identical to that of the wild tiger. The wild one gave a little meat to the bleating tiger, who had difficulty eating it. Gradually, however, the grass eating tiger got to know the taste of blood, and came to relish the meat. Then the wild tiger said: "Now you see there is no difference between you and me; come along and follow me into the forest."[3]

We can well imagine the jungle reverberating sound of the two free tigers roaring! We have forgotten our face, our wild roar, and we bleat as if we were goats. When we remember ourselves, it is like the prodigal son when he came to himself. This our brother "was dead and is alive again, was lost and is found" (Luke 15:24). Miserable though we may be, we can come alive; we can reorient ourselves and undergo a radical transformation. With effort, knowledge, and guidance, one can become what one truly is, "Son of the Most High," partaker of Divine Nature, and a child of God (Psalm 82:6; II Peter 1:4; I John 3:1-2).

In samadhi the seeing is without subjectivity. Attention in the state of samadhi is free attention, freed from all constraints and all functions. Attention in this state is not conditioned by any object, even very subtle ones, such as ideas and feelings.

This stage is closer to that of being the beloved when Purusha, the Conscious Energy and Transcendent Being, is the sole initiator; all the elements of Prakriti in a human being—body, mind, feelings—are completely relaxed and receptive.

The three stages—dhyana, dharana, samadhi—are like those of a warrior, lover and beloved—in the movement from the ego to the Self or to God.

3.4

त्रयमेकत्र संयमः

trayam-ekatra saṃyamaḥ

Total attention (*samyama*) is when dharana, dhyana, and samadhi are together.

3.5

तज्जयात्प्रज्ञालोकः

taj-jayāt prajñā-ālokaḥ

The illumination of insight results from the mastery of this.

3.6

तस्य भूमिषु विनियोगः

tasya bhūmiṣu viniyogaḥ

The practice of samyama is accomplished gradually.

3.7

त्रयमन्तरङ्गं पूर्वेभ्यः

trayam-antar-aṅgaṃ pūrvebhyaḥ

These three limbs of yoga are inner limbs with respect to the limbs discussed previously.

3.8

तदपि बहिरङ्गं निर्बीजस्य

tad-api bahir-aṅgaṃ nirbījasya

Still, these are external to nirbija samadhi.

Samyama, total attention, is realized when all three forms of attention—dharana, dhyana, and samadhi—are practiced together at the same time. This seems to be much like the "total attention" spoken of by Krishnamurti. In this state the splendor of insight emerges, and the person sees the suchness, the thing-in-itself (*ding en sich* of Immanuel Kant), of whatever the attention of samyama is directed upon.

This is a state of pure consciousness, a state totally empty of my ego self but full of Purusha, the Conscious Energy. Purusha is wholly other (*totaliter aliter*) than anything that can be known. But it is intimately my Self; the Highest and Unknowable God resides in my deepest, in its true form.[4] "Look within, you are the Buddha" said the Enlightened One.

Samyama attention is the entry to direct insight. With this attention, we can see into the nature of reality. Like any other process, it is accomplished in stages, even though the precise moments of insight are like quantum jumps and cannot be mapped in time.

Even though the three limbs of dharana, dhyana, and samadhi are internal to the other five limbs of yoga, it is now said that these three are external compared with nirbija samadhi, contemplation without seed. The process described so far—including dharana, dhyana, and samadhi and their composite, samyama—is concerned with the quieting of vrittis, the contents of consciousness. When the mind is cleansed, then it is possible to know without the interference of the categories of the mind and to gain the knowledge of the noumenon. In what follows, Patañjali discusses the transformation of the structure of consciousness, which is more like a transmutation of the mind, as in a species change.

After this transmutation, there will be a new birth—the birth of a radically new person with new being, "born, not of blood, nor of carnal will, nor by man's desire, but of God" (John 1:13).

All spiritual practice is for this inner birth. Meister Eckhart said, "A Christian is called to be Mary and to give birth to the Word."

Transformations of the Mind

3.9

व्युत्थाननिरोधसंस्कारयोरभिभवप्रादुर्भावौ निरोधक्षणचित्तान्वयो निरोधपरिणामः

vyutthāna-nirodha-saṃskārayor-abhibhava-prādur-bhāvau nirodha-kṣaṇa-chitta-anvayo nirodha-pariṇāmaḥ

Nirodha parinama, transformation towards silence, is the transformation of the mind in which the attention moves from the rise and fall of the external impressions to the silence which pervades when the mind is settled.

3.10

तस्य प्रशान्तवाहितासंस्कारात्

tasya praśānta-vāhitā saṃskārāt

The flow of silence becomes constant from the internal impressions of this quiet.

3.11

सर्वार्थतैकाग्रतयोः क्षयोदयौ चित्तस्य समाधिपरिणामः

sarva-arthatā-ekāgratayoḥ kṣaya-udayau chittasya samādhi-pariṇāmaḥ

Samadhi parinama, transformation towards realization, is the gradual settling of distractions and the simultaneous rising of one-pointedness.

3.12

ततः पुनः शान्तोदितौ तुल्यप्रत्ययौ चित्तस्यैकाग्रतापरिणामः

tataḥ punaḥ śānta-uditau tulya-pratyayau chittasya-ekāgratā-pariṇāmaḥ

Ekagrata parinama, transformation towards one-pointedness, is the stage of transformation in which activity and silence are equally balanced in the mind.

Various transformations of the mind, or of consciousness, are spoken about in the above sutras. These are transformations in the material substratum of Prakriti, both inside the mind as well as outside it. This constitutes the basis of the miraculous knowledge that can be obtained by performing samyama on different parts of the organism.

The one-pointedness mentioned in the sutra (3.12) above is not a focusing of the mind as in dharana, but it is a one-pointed directionality of attention, a constancy and a steadiness, towards the flow of silence. All the three kinds of transformations (*parinama*) mentioned above—nirodha, samadhi, and ekagrata—have to do with the relationship between the impressions coming from outside and the underlying silence of a still mind. In the nirodha parinama, the attention moves repeatedly from the disturbance created by an impression to the silence of the mind. In the samadhi parinama, there is a gradual diminishing of the distractions caused by the impressions and an increasing orientation to the silence of the mind. In the ekagrata parinama, there is a balancing of the impressions and the silence; the impressions are received in the mind but the fundamental underlying silence remains. That is closer to a transmutation of the structure of the mind, a new birth and a new being. As Plotinus says of a transformed person, "this man has now become another and is neither himself nor his own" (*Enneads* vi 9.10).

The sages who have undergone this kind of radical transformation have a different quality of mind. It seemed obviously true in the case of Krishnamurti. I was struck by the special nature and quality of Krishnamurti's mind, so I often asked him about the particularities of his mind.

He frequently spoke about the religious mind and its innocence, freshness and vulnerability. He would often suggest that he was just like everybody else and not someone special. But I was never convinced of this. On one occasion, when I persisted in asking about the nature of his extraordinary mind, he said, "Sir, do you think the speaker is a freak?" Freak or not, he certainly was extraordinary and unusual. As was mentioned earlier, his mind was like a mill-pond; any disturbance that was created in it by an external stimulus soon died down, leaving it unruffled as before.

Patañjali tells us that the whole difference between an ordinary person and an accomplished yogi is in the quality and depth of the silence of mind and how soon this silence returns after an external impression is received.

3.13

एतेन भूतेन्द्रियेषु धर्मलक्षणावस्थापरिणामा व्याख्याताः

etena bhūta-indriyeṣu dharma-lakṣaṇa-avasthā-pariṇāmā vyākhyātāḥ

By extension, the transformations of the mind explain the transformations of material nature—transformations of quality, form, and state.

3.14

शान्तोदिताव्यपदेश्यधर्मानुपाती धर्मी

śānta-udita-avyapadeśya-dharma-anupātī dharmī

The substratum underlying the essential properties of material nature endures whether these properties are at rest, arising, or unmanifest.

3.15

क्रमान्यत्वं परिणामान्यत्वे हेतुः

krama-anyatvaṃ pariṇāma-anyatve hetuḥ

Variations in the sequence of properties cause differences in the transformation of material nature.

After mentioning the three kinds of transformation of the mind, Patañjali makes the somewhat startling comment that these very transformations also apply to the transformation of material nature. As the mind undergoes the three transformations mentioned above, there are transformations of the quality, form, and state of the objects of samyama corresponding to those. Even though the underlying material essence of the object remains unchanged, the quality, form, and the state of the material can be changed corresponding to the transformations of the mind. This is the basis of the miraculous powers described further in this chapter of the *Yoga Sutras* that an advanced yogi can acquire over the objects of attention.

▪ Subtle Knowledge

3.16

परिणामत्रयसंयमादतीतानागतज्ञानम्

pariṇāma-traya-saṃyamād-atīta-anāgata-jñānam

By samyama on the three kinds of transformations (*nirodha*, *samadhi*, *ekagrata*) knowledge of the past and of the future can be gained.

3.17

शब्दार्थप्रत्ययानामितरेतराध्यासात्
संकरस्तत्प्रविभागसंयमात्सर्वभूतरुतज्ञानम्

śabda-artha-praṭyayānām-itara-itara-adhyāsāt-saṃkaras-tat-pravibhāga-saṃyamāt-sarva-bhūta-ruta-jñānam

Understanding of an object is usually confused because the name, the meaning, and the perception of the object are mistakenly identified. Through samyama on the distinction among these three, the knowledge of the sound of all beings can be gained.

3.18

संस्कारसाक्षात्करणात्पूर्वजातिज्ञानम्

saṃskāra-sākṣāt-karaṇāt-pūrva-jāti-jñānam

Knowledge of previous births can be gained from direct perception of samskaras.

The basic principle underlying this discussion is that in a fully developed person, the microcosmos (*kshudra brahmanda*) mirrors the megalocosmos (*brahmanda*). Many *vibhutis* (powers, manifestations, phenomena) accompany the yogic journey; they are not a separate issue. They cannot be denied and need not be ignored. In fact, the kinds of knowledge which are mentioned here may be needed by a master to help students or for other purposes. However, increased powers bring greater responsibilities; therefore, the attitude to these powers is of paramount importance.

The ability to bring samyama attention is an indication of a highly developed consciousness. These powers are not something which are available to the lower level mind. The right use of such powers requires a developed will, great insight, and enormous compassion. If powers are acquired (through sadhana or through magic, or drugs, or will), they can be misused if there is not a continuing work towards freedom from the ego and its greed and self-importance. We all have powers and talents which we can use and whatever is true about more unusual powers is also true about the powers we already have. What is the right use of these powers? What is required of us in order not to misuse what we have been given?

Patañjali has said more than once that the combination of tapas, svadhyaya, and Ishvara pranidhana is the way to invite Purusha, the sole seer, to see through our organism. Tapas is the self-discipline required to persist with our undertaking, to stay in front of the object of our search, to make an effort and not to give up. In Ishvara pranidhana we are reminded that there are higher and larger forces and that we need to be in accord with them. Ishvara pranidhana is not a dedication to a particular form of God, but to the higher and more conscious energies within the universe and within ourselves. It is only possible when I realize that I am not the crown of creation and that the universe was not made for me. Ishvara is seated within each one of us, as Krishna repeatedly says in the Bhagavad Gita, but this subtle energy is not exclusively mine or yours. Ishvara is at the very center of myself, but Ishvara is everywhere, at the center of every being. Its center is everywhere and its circumference nowhere.

Our self includes the whole range, from the isolated and exclusive ego-self to the highest Self which is identical with Brahman. And spiritual development has to do with what part in this spectrum from the isolated ego-self to the Self we are identified with. Although there is a repeated reminder in the Gurdjieff teaching that we human beings are afflicted with self-love and that this is one of the greatest obstacles in our search, yet on one occasion Madame de Salzmann said, "You don't love your self enough, the Self that wishes and needs to emerge." We need repeatedly to turn to svadhyaya—self-knowledge, self-study, self-observation, self-realization—more and more impartially, without fear and self-importance.

Attention is the main power of transformation. Transformation is not brought about by a decision of our ordinary mind, nor by any efforts arising from the level of consciousness which needs to be transformed. Seeing is at a level higher than what is seen, and therefore it can bring about a transformation in the quality of what is seen. Seeing the way it is in myself, steadily and impartially, brings about a transformation of myself. I need to acknowledge myself, accept myself, and love myself—ego and all—without manipulation, without himsa. I cannot love another, or be compassionate to another, unless I accept myself and am compassionate to myself. If I am not right by myself, I cannot be right by anyone else or by God. The whole range of myself needs to be acknowledged. To truly see "what is" transforms "what is" in actuality to "What Is" in reality.

As the sutras above say, to understand the change involved in transformation is to understand time sequence. The Greek word *physis* which is translated as "nature" means "change." The whole natural world is dynamic; change is a constant feature of everything which exists in time. By understanding the laws which govern change, past and future can be understood. This has been the undertaking of science, but the laws governing subtler and non-physical levels of reality require a subtler science such as yoga.

How do we understand an object? Is the understanding obtained by hearing the name of the object, the label attached to it? Does the understanding arise from knowing the meaning of the words used to describe something? Or from a perception of the object? The name of something is not the same as the thing itself, nor the same as the perception of the thing. We can falsely assume that we know something because we have heard the description in words, either from having heard them, or read them or from memory. The meaning of an experience or an object is not necessarily what we think, or what others say, but needs to be received with an open mind. Usually we speak of the meaning of words, but objects and experiences also have meanings, which includes their intention, purpose and significance. The sutras above suggest that if we pay total attention (samyama) to the differences among the name of an object, the meaning of that object and the perception of it, we can begin to hear the subtler vibrations behind the words and then we can understand the language of animals, other human beings and of angels. Listening with a silent mind, without its chatter, is difficult but necessary.

In the sutra (3.18) above, the Sanskrit word *sakshatkara* which means "direct perception" is used in much the same way as samyama. This indicates something of the quality of samyama, perfect discipline and total attention. It is much closer to a direct look at something without the distractions of the mind than thinking about that thing. By a direct perception of our latent tendencies or predispositions, we can gain knowledge of our previous births in which these tendencies were formed. This knowing is not for the sake of gaining information about past lives in a historical sense, but for the sake of knowing ourselves at depth.

3.19

प्रत्ययस्य परचित्तज्ञानम्

pratyayasya para-chitta-jñānam

Through direct perception of their intention, knowledge of another's mind can be gained.

3.20

न च तत्सालम्बनं तस्याविषयीभूतत्वात्

na cha tat-sa-ālambanaṃ tasya-aviṣayī-bhūtatvāt

This does not involve knowledge of the underlying object of thought since that is not in one's field of perception.

3.21

कायरूपसंयमात्तद्ग्राह्यशक्तिस्तम्भे चक्षुः
प्रकाशासंप्रयोगेऽन्तर्धानम्

kāya-rūpa-saṃyamāt-tad-grāhya-śakti-stambhe chakṣuḥ-prakāśa-a-saṃprayoge' ntardhānam

From samyama on the form of the body, by breaking the contact between the eye of the observer and the light reflected by the body, the body becomes invisible.

3.22

सोपक्रमं निरुपक्रमं च कर्म तत्संयमादपरान्तज्ञानमरिष्टेभ्यो वा

sa-upakramaṃ nir-upakramaṃ cha karma tat-saṃyamād-apara-anta-jñānam-ariṣṭebhyo vā

From samyama on the immediate and remote effects of action (karma) foreknowledge of death can be gained.

3.23

मैत्र्यादिषु बलानि

maitry-ādiṣu balāni

From samyama on friendliness and similar qualities, these qualities can be gained.

3.24

बलेषु हस्तिबलादीनि

baleṣu hasti-bala-ādīni

From samyama on the strength of an animal, such as an elephant, one gains that strength.

3.25

प्रवृत्त्यालोकन्यासात्सूक्ष्मव्यवहित विप्रकृष्टज्ञानम्

pravṛtty-āloka-nyāsāt sūkṣma-vyavahita-viprakṛṣṭa-jñānam

Knowledge of the subtle, the concealed and the remote can be achieved by directing the inner light.

3.26

भुवनज्ञानं सूर्ये संयमात्

bhuvana-jñānaṃ sūrye saṃyamāt

Knowledge of the universe can be gained by samyama on the sun.

3.27

चन्द्रे ताराव्यूहज्ञानम्

chandre tārā-vyūha-jñānam

Knowledge of the arrangement of the stars can be gained by samyama on the moon.

3.28

ध्रुवे तद्गतिज्ञानम्

dhruve tad-gati-jñānam

Knowledge of the movement of the stars can be gained by samyama on the polar star.

3.29

नाभिचक्रे कायव्यूहज्ञानम्

nābhi-chakre kāya-vyūha-jñānam

Knowledge of the bodily system can be gained by samyama on the navel center.

3.30

कण्ठकूपे क्षुत्पिपासानिवृत्तिः

kaṇṭha-kūpe kṣut-pipāsā-nivṛttiḥ

Hunger and thirst can be overcome by samyama on the throat hollow.

3.31

कूर्मनाड्यां स्थैर्यम्

kūrma-nāḍyāṃ sthairyam

Stability can be achieved by samyama on the *kurma nadi* (tortoise vein).

3.32

मूर्धज्योतिषि सिद्धदर्शनम्

mūrdha-jyotiṣi siddha-darśanam

Samyama on the light in the head brings vision of perfected beings.

3.33

प्रातिभाद्वा सर्वम्

prātibhād-vā sarvam

And, knowledge of the all can be reached through intuitive perception.

3.34

हृदये चित्तसंवित्

hṛdaye chitta-saṃvit

Samyama on the heart leads to an understanding of chitta.

Changing the scale of perception—as we do with a microscope or a telescope—is different from changing the level of perception. As William Blake says, "What a sage sees is not what an ordinary person sees." The perception of the Buddha, a third-eye perception, is different in quality from our perception.

A master of yoga can become invisible by affecting the consciousness of the perceiver. At a much lower level, we know that in hypnosis a person can be given a suggestion not to see the things or the events which are objectively there, and to see some things which are not there.

Several sutras above, especially 3.25-29, give some hints of the yogic method of research into natural phenomena. The principle of analogy or isomorphism between one thing—nearby or within ourselves—and another which could be remote, is a fundamental premise of traditional knowledge. In particular, the human being mirrors the cosmos. With a sensitive and sustained observation (samyama) it is possible to know the laws which govern the processes in ourselves and in others, but also by analogy the laws in larger spheres. The method practiced by a yogi to study the cosmos is through self-study without self-occupation.

Another principle which is suggested here is the holographic principle according to which if a part is known the whole can be known. For example, as is said in sutra 3.28-30, knowledge of the movement of the stars can be gained by samyama on the polar star, and knowledge of the bodily system can be gained by samyama on the navel center.

Knowledge leads to power; but it can lead to black magic if it is not accompanied by a fully developed conscience. All the great sages have warned against being fascinated by the magical powers which somewhat naturally develop on the spiritual journey. One can fall at any stage of development. Lucifer was the highest of all angels, closest to the Almighty, but in his hubris he wanted to be like the Most High, and was banished from heaven. Similarly, Ravana, the titanic demonic figure in the *Ramayana*, the most ancient epic of India, was such a learned man that he is shown with ten heads. He was a great devotee of Shiva and because of his austerities he had won all sorts of powers and protections. But because of one fundamental flaw in his character, that of pride and self-importance, he became a great tyrant and had to be killed by Rama, an incarnation of Vishnu. In the right development of a human being, development of conscience needs to precede the development of consciousness. No doubt this is the reason why yama and niyama are placed by Patañjali as the first two limbs of his eight-limbed yoga.

Miraculous Powers

Siddhis as Impediments

3.35

सत्त्वपुरुषयोरत्यन्तासंकीर्णयोः प्रत्ययाविशेषो भोगः
परार्थात्वात्स्वार्थसंयमात्पुरुषज्ञानम्

sattva-puruṣayor-atyanta-asaṃkīrṇayoḥ pratyaya-aviśeṣobhogaḥ para-arthātvāt sva-artha-saṃyamāt-puruṣa-jñānam

When the quality of perfect sattva is close to the quality of Purusha, experience serves Purusha. By samyama on the purposes of perfect sattva, one gains insight into Purusha.

3.36

ततः प्रातिभश्रावणवेदनादर्शास्वादवार्ता जायन्ते

tataḥ prātibha-śrāvaṇa-vedanā-ādarśa-āsvāda-vārtā jāyante

Thus, subtle hearing, touching, seeing, tasting, and smelling are born.

3.37

ते समाधावुपसर्गा व्युत्थाने सिद्धयः

te samādhāv-upasargā vyutthāne siddhayaḥ

These powers (*siddhis*) are attainments in the world, but they are impediments to samadhi.

Again and again, Patañjali returns to the question of the right relationship between Purusha and Prakriti, between Atman and *sharira* (body), between spirit and matter, between God and the world. In general, we are lost in the world or in the comforts and pleasures of the body-mind. How can we understand the right place and function of the body-mind? How can we see God in the world? How can we have some relationship with God? How can we come to a realization of the real Self, the true I, in this body?

The first time Madame de Salzmann said to me, "Your body is not only yours" I was completely perplexed. Who else or what else could have a stake in my body? Gradually it began to be clear to me in feeling that something higher than what I usually call myself has taken on my body-mind for some purpose, and that the body exists for that. I began to understand that if my body does not serve a higher purpose, then this incarnation is wasted.

Madame de Salzmann added, "The Lord, the Seigneur, is there, but he needs my body to come. The body is not ready. It needs to be prepared. If the mind and the body are connected, then the higher energy, which is what religions call Seigneur, will appear. It cannot be done easily or cheaply. But it must be done. It is necessary for the maintenance of our world. The body has to serve something else, not itself. The body itself is designed for destruction; it has to serve something else."

It is a lesson of all the great traditions that without God it cannot be done, but without human beings it will not be done. We need to play our part in welcoming God to work through us.

There is no suggestion in the sutras above that experience is a bad thing or that it is undesirable. Experience constitutes life and being alive means that we experience. However, in order to serve Purusha, the spiritual element which is incarnated in the body, we need to be very clear about the distinction between Purusha and Prakriti so that we do not confuse the rider with the vehicle. According to Patañjali, Purusha is always the subject; it cannot be an object of knowledge. Whatever can be an object of knowledge, however refined and subtle, is not Purusha. But Purusha needs the purified mind—of the nature of sattva, the clearest aspect of Prakriti—to know itself. As Meister Eckhart said, "God cannot know himself without me." In one hadith, a divine saying in Islam, Allah says, "I was a hidden Treasure and I loved to be known. So I created humanity—and the other creatures—that I might be known."

We cannot know Purusha, but Purusha can know itself through us. "Self alone knows the Self," said Aristotle. Whatever can be known is not God. Purusha cannot be known; it is the knower. Still the sutra says that by samyama on the purpose of Purusha as distinct from the purpose of Prakriti, which is to serve Purusha, leads to Purusha jñana. Jñana, as it occurs in the sutra (3.35) above, is usually translated as "knowledge." How can there be knowledge of Purusha? Jñana is not knowledge by separation in which subject and object remain distinct; it is "knowledge," or rather gnosis, by participation, by the fusion of subject and object. It is a knowing which is the same as becoming. The kind of insight that can lead us to the Spirit has a transforming character; in the process we become different. In order to know what is higher than us, we have to be higher. In fact, being and knowing are so intimately connected that the Mundaka Upanishad (3.2.9) declares, "*Brahmanvid brahmaiva bhavati:* One who knows Brahman becomes Brahman." For Parmenides (*Diels*, Fr. 185) and Plotinus (*Enneads* vi. 9) "to be and to know are one and the same." Opening oneself to the Spirit is thus already a movement towards being born of the Spirit.

It is possible to think of Purusha as consciousness; but we must not confuse consciousness with the contents of consciousness. The contents of consciousness and Purusha are not the same. Purusha is pure consciousness.

Bringing the attention of samyama on the purposes of Purusha leads to the enhancement of all the senses—seeing, smelling, tasting, hearing, and touching—and an increased sensitivity discloses hidden and remote objects. Masters of yoga can acquire powers of clairaudience and clairvoyance, which is to say they can hear at a distance or see at a distance.

Patañjali has nothing against magical or occult powers; to him they are a natural extension of the senses. When asked about these miraculous powers, Madame de Salzmann said, "There are no miracles. It is all a play of forces." However, she warned against using these powers for egotistic purposes. This is a precaution given by all the great teachers, including Patañjali, the Buddha and the Christ. Superpowers can present the greatest temptations for an aspirant; if these powers or these enhanced senses are turned outward and used for worldly success or control over others, then they become impediments to samadhi. We can appreciate again the necessity of practicing yamas and niyamas, the first two limbs of yoga in order to develop a clearer conscience as we work for greater consciousness and will.

Even at the highest stages of spiritual development, self importance or egotistic ambition can arise, tempting a yogi to use the occult powers for manipulating the world for selfish purposes. Lucifer was the highest of all angels, nearest to God, but pride and ambition got hold of him and he was expelled from heaven. "How art thou fallen from heaven, O Lucifer, son of the morning! How art thou cut down to the ground . . . For thou hast said in thine heart, I will ascend into heaven, I will exalt my throne above the stars of God . . . I will ascend above the heights of the clouds; I will be like the most High" (Isaiah 14:12-14).

▪ Mastery over Natural Forces

3.38

बन्धकारणशैथिल्यात्प्रचारसंवेदनाच्च चित्तस्य परशरीरावेशः

bandha-kāraṇa-śaithilyāt-prachāra-saṃvedanāch-cha chittasya para-śarīra-āveśaḥ

Being free of the sources of bondage, perceiving the manifestations of another, one is able to enter their body through consciousness.

3.39

उदानजयाज्जलपङ्कण्टकादिष्वसङ्ग उत्क्रान्तिश्च

udāna-jayāj-jala-paṅka-kaṇṭaka-ādiṣv-asaṅga utkrāntiś-cha

From the mastery of the movement of subtle breath rising in the body, one is freed from being caught by mud, thorns, and water, and one can rise above them.

Several supreme powers (*siddhis*) which result from samyama, total attention, on various aspects of Prakriti are described in this chapter. Generally these siddhis are ascribed to the physical body (*sthula sharira*), but it is more reasonable to assume that they belong to the subtle body (*sukshma sharira*). There are eight siddhis which are associated with advanced yogis. According to the *Yoga Bhashya*[5] of Vyasa these are:

1. *Animan*: atomization, miniaturization of the body. By this siddhi a yogi can make the body very small.

2. *Mahiman*: magnification, the power to expand infinitely. This power is just the opposite of the previous one and a yogi can appear very large if needed.

3. *Laghiman*: levitation. An outstanding example of this power is presented by St. Teresa of Avilla. She did not ask for this power nor did she wish it. It is said that she was often bothered by levitation while sweeping the floor in her monastery and she would pray to God to free her of this nuisance.

4. *Prapti*: extension, the power to reach everywhere. An example of this power can be found in a remark of Meister Eckhart: "Yesterday I said something that would seem truly incredible. I said: Jerusalem is as near to my soul as the place where I am now standing. Yes, in all truth; what is even more than a thousand miles farther than Jerusalem is as near to my soul as my own body; and I am as sure of this as I am of being a man."

5. *Prakamya*: freedom of will. Most of us assume that human beings have free will. However, this siddhi implies that ordinarily we do not have free will. We are very much conditioned by our species, culture, family, and by the past in general. Even a spiritually developed person like St. Paul can have a divided will which results in a lack of freedom and self-control. "I do not even acknowledge my own actions as mine, for what I do is not what I want to do, but what I detest," says St. Paul. "The good which I want to do, I fail to do; but what I do is the wrong which is against my will" (Romans 7:15, 20). Similarly, Arjuna asks in the Bhagavad Gita (3:36), "Krishna, what is it that makes a man do evil, even against his own will; under compulsion, as it were?" It is rare for a human being to have free will; however, an advanced yogi who is freed of all conditioning can have free will and be able to act freshly without the constraints of the past.

6. *Vashitva*: mastery over the entire creation. This siddhi is a continuation of the idea that those who wish to possess nothing and do not hanker after anything, will have all that they need without their asking. Thus they become masters of the whole world.

7. *Ishitritva*: the power of creation. This is the power which in mythology is attributed to Brahma, the god of creation in the Hindu Trinity of Brahma, Vishnu, and Shiva, where Vishnu is the preserver and therefore the god of Dharma, and Shiva is the transformer, the god of dance, theater, music, grammar, and yoga. All the gods in the Trinity have their feminine counterparts—Sarasvati, Lakshmi, and Shakti, respectively—and it is with the help of the feminine energies that they carry out their functions. The creator god, Brahma, has the goddess of wisdom, Sarasvati, as his consort. A yogi who has great wisdom acquires the siddhi of ishitritva and is able to create whatever is needed.

8. *Kamavasayitva*: the power of wish fulfillment. It is often said in the Indian tradition that the whole universe is like a wish

fulfilling tree (*kalpavriksha*) or a wish granting cow (*kamadhenu*), but that our wishes and desires are generally chaotic and self-contradictory. In a developed yogi, wish is more unified and consistent with the universal forces.

3.40

समानजयाज्ज्वलनम्

samāna-jayāj-jvalanam

Radiance is the result of mastery of the movement of the mid-breath.

In the sutra above, Patañjali speaks of the radiance produced by samyama on *samana*, breath in the middle region of the body. The breath (*prana*) is intimately related with the spirit in many traditions. In Japan, the center of the body and the soul in a person is called *hara* and this center is given a particular emphasis in many spiritual disciplines of Japan, and especially in Zen Buddhism where it is maintained that anyone not centered in the hara is not centered at all. This center is in the belly, below the solar plexus. This designation itself is suggestive of the great importance attached to the solar plexus, for the spirit is symbolized by the sun in many traditions. The center is near the navel which physically is the place for the inflow of the life-sustaining energies through the umbilical cord. In the theory of yoga, one of the very important *chakras* (centers of energy) is located near the navel. It is called the *manipura chakra* which literally means the center which is filled with jewels.

The seat of the spirit in the sutra is identified with the belly (Greek *koilia*), in keeping with many spiritual traditions, including the Hebraic. One finds in Proverbs (20:27), "The breath of man is the lamp of the Lord, searching all the inner parts of his belly."

"On the last and the greatest day of the festival Jesus stood and cried aloud: 'If anyone thirsts, let him come; let him drink who believes in me.'" As Scripture says, "From his belly rivers of living water shall flow" (John 7:37-38).

3.41

श्रोत्राकाशयोः संबन्धसंयमाद्दिव्यं श्रोत्रम

śrotra-ākāśayoḥ saṃbandha-saṃyamād-divyaṃ śrotram

The divine ear develops with samyama on the connection between ear and space.

3.42

कायाकाशयोः संबन्धसंयमाल्लघुतूल समापत्तेश्चाकाशगमनम्

kāya-ākāśayoḥ saṃbandha-saṃyamāl-laghu-tūla-samāpatteś-cha-ākāśa-gamanam

From samyama on the connection between the body and space and by samapatti with the lightness of cotton, one can move through space at will.

3.43

बहिरकल्पिता वृत्तिर्महाविदेहा ततः प्रकाशावरणक्षयः

bahir-akalpitā vṛttir-mahā-videhā tataḥ prakāśa-āvaraṇa-kṣayaḥ

The veil covering the light within is destroyed by contacting the state of consciousness which is beyond the body and is inconceivable.

3.44

स्थूलस्वरूपसूक्ष्मान्वयार्थवत्त्वसंयमाद् भूतजयः

sthūla-sva-rūpa-sūkṣma-anvaya-arthavattva-saṃyamād-bhūta-jayaḥ

From samyama on gross, intrinsic, subtle, relational, and purposive aspects of the elements of matter, one attains mastery over them.

3.45

ततोऽणिमादिप्रादुर्भावः कायसम्पत्तद्धर्मानभिघातश्च

tato' ṇima-ādi-prādurbhāvaḥ kāya-saṃpat-tad-dharma-anabhighātaś-cha

Then extraordinary powers appear, such as the power to be as small as an atom, as well as bodily perfection and indestructibility.

3.46

रूपलावण्यबलवज्रसंहननत्वानि कायसम्पत

rūpa-lāvaṇya-bala-vajra-saṃhananatvāni kāya-saṃpat

Perfection of the body is expressed in beauty of form, vigor, strength, and firm stability.

3.47

ग्रहणस्वरूपास्मितान्वयार्थवत्त्वसंयमादिन्द्रियजयः

grahaṇa-sva-rūpa-asmitā-anvaya-arthavattva-saṃyamād-indriya-jayaḥ

Samyama on the real nature of the senses and their process of perception and of identification with the separate self leads to mastery over the senses.

3.48

ततो मनोजवित्वं विकरणभावः प्रधानजयश्च

tato mano-javitvaṃ vikaraṇa-bhāvaḥ pradhāna-jayaś-cha

From this one acquires quickness of mind, super-sensual perception and mastery over primordial matter.

3.49

सत्त्वपुरुषान्यताख्यातिमात्रस्य सर्वभावाधिष्ठातृत्वं सर्वज्ञातृत्वं च

sattva-puruṣa-anyatā-khyāti-mātrasya sarva-bhāva-adhiṣṭhātṛtvaṃ sarva-jñātṛtvaṃ cha

Knowledge of all and sovereignty over all are achieved from a discernment of the difference between sattva and Purusha.

In the sutra (3.41) above the development of *divya shrotram*, the divine ear, is mentioned. When Krishna shows his great form to Arjuna, he says, "O Arjuna, now behold the entire creation; animate, inanimate, and whatever else you like to see; all at one place in my body. But, you are not able to see Me with your physical eye; therefore, I give you *divya chakshu* (a divine eye) to see my majestic power and glory" (Bhagavad Gita 11:7-8).

We can understand from this parallel that it is not only a matter of clairaudience or clairvoyance, but also of subtle hearing and seeing. With the divya shrotram one can hear the voice of the silence, or the *anahata nada*, soundless sound which the sages have said fills the whole universe.

In the other sutras above many other powers and accomplishments are mentioned. Patañjali places an enormous importance on making a clear distinction between Purusha and Prakriti, or between the Self and non-Self, as the Vedantists would say. Discernment of the difference is not in order to separate the two but to discover the right relationship between them. By sustained discernment (*viveka*) and the clear vision (*khyati*), the right order and the proper relationship between Purusha and sattva, the most refined aspect of Prakriti, will arise. It is not that a yogi would then have personal sovereignty over Prakriti; it is more that Purusha has the sovereignty through the yogi whose consciousness as well as conscience are purified, and who has freedom from the ego and from all selfishness.

Unconditioned Freedom

3.50

तद्वैराग्यादपि दोषबीजक्षये कैवल्यम्

tad-vairāgyād-api doṣa-bīja-kṣaye kaivalyam

Vairagya even from this destroys the seed of bondage and leads to Kaivalya (freedom without measure).

3.51

स्थान्युपनिमन्त्रणे सङ्गस्मयाकरणं पुनरनिष्टप्रसङ्गात्

sthāny-upanimantraṇe saṅga-smaya-akaraṇaṃ punar-aniṣṭa-prasaṅgāt

One should not respond with pleasure or pride to the alluring invitations of exalted beings lest harmful attachment recur.

3.52

क्षणतत्क्रमयोः संयमाद्विवेकजं ज्ञानम्

kṣaṇa-tat-kramayoḥ saṃyamād-viveka-jaṃ jñānam

From samyama on the moment of time and on time sequence, jñana born of viveka, insight born of discernment, is gained.

3.53

जातिलक्षणदेशैरन्यतानवच्छेदात् तुल्ययोस्ततः प्रतिपत्तिः

jāti-lakṣaṇa-deśair-anyatā-anavachchhedāt-tulyayos-tataḥ pratipattiḥ

Through discernment one realizes the different origins, characteristics, and positions which distinguish two seemingly similar things.

3.54

तारकं सर्वविषयं सर्वथाविषयमक्रमं चेति विवेकजं ज्ञानम्

tārakaṃ sarva-viṣayaṃ sarvathā-viṣayam-akramaṃ cha-iti viveka-jaṃ jñānam

This jñana born of viveka is liberating, comprehensive, eternal, and freed of time sequence.

3.55

सत्त्वपुरुषयोः शुद्धिसाम्ये कैवल्यमिति

sattva-puruṣayoḥ śuddhi-sāmye kaivalyam-iti

When sattva and Purusha are equal in purity, Kaivalya is there. It is thus.

Kaivalya is the aloneness of seeing, or pure perception. It is achieved—or we should rather say that it is arrived at, or it arrives—by vairagya towards even the most subtle satisfactions, experiences and powers.

High beings, such as devas or angels, can offer all sorts of pleasures and comforts of heaven or paradise. Hearing subtle truths, being able to do magical things, or being an important person, are all temptations of the ego. These exalted celestial beings are as much within ourselves as outside. This was a realization of Siddhartha as he became Buddha (awake, discerning, enlightened); he saw that Mara, the tempter, was a projection of his own yearnings. Patañjali warns against these allurements, not because they do not exist, but because they are not Purusha which is the aim of our sadhana. We can be waylaid in our quest by falling into self-pride and by becoming attached to the experiences and powers which accompany any inner development.

Time sequence and spatial distance are transcended in the state of Kaivalya, and all happenings are present to Purusha, the Transcendent Conscious Energy, simultaneously. The insight gained in the state of Kaivalya is comprehensive, eternal and nonsequential. All events are present at once. Above all, this insight is liberating, for it is free of all bondage and free of the kleshas.

Prakriti fulfills her purpose when she allows Purusha to see and act through her without distortion. All spiritual practice is for this inner reorientation in which the body fulfills its purpose by serving the Spirit. As was quoted earlier, Meister Eckhart said, "Every Christian is called to be Mary and give to birth to the Word."

It is sometimes said that for a yogi in a state of samadhi, Prakriti ceases to dance. It is closer to the truth to say that the dance of Prakriti ceases to assert a hold on the yogi's attention. The *Yoga Sutras* represents a continuation of the Vedic yajña (sacrifice). It is said in the Rig Veda that yajña is the navel of the cosmos around which everything turns (I.164.35). Sacrifice is at the heart of all spiritual practice; this is how our life is made sacred. Here, in the recurring metaphor in the *Yoga Sutras*, the entire realm of the visible (Prakriti) is submitted for the power to see (Purusha); thus the whole manifestation of Prakriti becomes sacred.

Sacrifice is also at the heart of the process of transmission of a teaching. This point has been emphasized by Sri Anirvan: "One touches here a state of deep spiritual existentialism which is the eternal present. But every time one speaks about it, one destroys something of the power that is in action, for instead of interiorizing it, one exteriorizes it. That is why a Master who has accepted the task of teaching is sacrificing himself."[6] Every parent is aware of the sacrifice necessary for the birth, nurturing, and spiritual growth of a child. A real guru is like a parent who is related with the disciple through many trials. It is said in the Indian tradition that the physical birth takes place in the womb of the mother, but the spiritual birth is in the womb of the heart of the guru.

In the state of Kaivalya, Purusha, the real Self, the sole Knower and Seer, matches the vibration of the subtlest product of Prakriti, refined consciousness, the purest sattva. Then there is the aloneness of seeing, and a fusion of seeing, seer, and seen.

> *Except for the point, the still point,*
> *There would be no dance, and there is only the dance.*
> —"Burnt Norton" in *The Four Quartets* by T. S. Eliot

Endnotes:

1 In the movement of Buddhism from India "Dhyana" became "Ch'an" in China, "Sôn" in Korea, "Thôn" in Vietnam, and "Zen" in Japan.

2 The four great utterances are: "Thou art that" (*tat tvam asi*) Chhandogya Upanishad 6:8.7; "This Atman is Brahman" (*ayam atma brahman*) Mandukya Upanishad 2; "I am Brahman" (*aham brahmasmi*) Brihadaranyaka Upanishad 1.4:10; and "Consciousness is Brahman" (*prajñanam brahman*) Aitareya Upanishad 3:3.

3 *The Gospel of Shri Ramakrishna*, Translated with an introduction by Swami Nikhilananda (Madras: Mylapore, 1947), p. 170.

4 To refer to the Highest God in a neuter grammatical form is not meant to suggest that it is not developed enough to have a gender, as is the custom in English language; on the contrary, far from being sub-gender it is so developed that it is super gender. Here a specification of gender, male or female, would be imposing a limitation.

5 As quoted by Georg Feuerstein, *The Yoga Sutra of Patañjali*, p. 118.

6 *To Live Within*, p. 151.

Kaivalya Pada

▪

Freedom Without Measure

Reality and Freedom

Subtle Impressions

4.1

जन्मौषधिमन्त्रतपः समाधिजाः सिद्धयः

janma-oṣadhi-mantra-tapaḥ-samādhi-jāḥ siddhayaḥ

Powers may be present at birth, or they may result from drugs, mantras, tapas, or samadhi.

A person can be born with the powers (siddhis) that were spoken of in the previous chapter of the *Yoga Sutras*, but they can also be cultivated by various means, such as by mantras, self-discipline, and by samadhi. This is also the case with talents. Child prodigies are born with unusual abilities, but talents can also be developed through practice and discipline. It is certainly borne out from historical evidence that some people have certain powers from childhood and regard them as quite natural. According to Patañjali, siddhis can also be cultivated with the use of herbs or drugs. This fact can lend itself to all sorts of misuse and fantasy. There have been cases in which people under the influence of LSD or other drugs have imagined that they can fly, and have jumped out of windows and have harmed themselves.

There is no suggestion anywhere in the yoga literature that seekers of truth can dispense with the strenuous work of self-discipline and can acquire these siddhis by taking drugs. Patañjali is not at all interested in pursuing the matter of siddhis any further, and there is no more mention of them. These powers are not the aim or purpose of yoga. The aim of yoga is a radical transformation of consciousness and the powers which are spoken of are a by-product of the discipline.

4.2

जात्यन्तरपरिणामः प्रकृत्यापूरात्

jāty-antara-pariṇāmaḥ prakṛty-āpūrāt

Transformation into a new state of being is the result of the fullness of the unfolding of the inherent potential of Prakriti.

4.3

निमित्तमप्रयोजकं प्रकृतीनां वरणभेदस्तु ततः क्षेत्रिकवत्

nimittam-aprayojakaṃ prakṛtīnāṃ-varaṇa-bhedas-tu tataḥ kṣetrikavat

The apparent causes of transformation do not in fact bring it about. They merely remove the obstacles to natural growth, as a farmer clears the ground for the crops.

From the first of the two sutras above, we see that revealing Purusha in its own true form is not against the purposes of Prakriti; in fact it is the fulfillment of the whole purpose of Prakriti. The transformation into a new being is a result of the unfolding of the inherent potential of Prakriti. As was discussed earlier, yoga practice is the reversal of the natural outward tendencies of Prakriti. But deep down everything in Prakriti wishes to serve the purposes of Purusha. It is therefore useful to return to the distinction between "higher nature" and "lower nature," or between "spiritual" and "carnal" nature. We are two natured, and yoga practice is against the tendencies of our lower nature, so that the tendencies of our higher nature can be supported. Pratiprasava is a reversal of the flow of the usual outward tendencies of Prakriti in order to aid the inward tendencies and aspirations.

Whatever we do from the lower mind, in the realm of thought and effort, cannot bring about transformation which comes only from above. However, effort and practice can prepare the ground by removing the obstacles, as a farmer helps the growth of the plants by removing the weeds.

Einstein, who was widely recognized as one of the most creative scientists of all times, was periodically asked about the nature and origin of creativity. On one occasion when he was asked whether creative work was ultimately a matter of hard work or of chance, he remarked, "Creativity is essentially a matter of chance; but chance seems to flavour the prepared."

Krishnamurti once said during a conversation with me that the intelligence beyond thought is just there, like the air, and does not need to be created by discipline or effort. "All one needs to do is to open the window." I suggested that most windows are painted shut and need a lot of scraping before they can be opened, and asked, "How does one scrape?" He did not wish to pursue this line of inquiry and closed it by saying, "You are too clever for your own good." But Patañjali provides practical help in preparing the body-mind so that the window of our consciousness can be opened. Purusha is just there, it does not need to be created; it cannot be created; however, purification of the instruments of perception in Prakriti allows Purusha to reveal itself.

The Sanskrit word *nimitta* in sutra 4.3 above is the occasion, or the instrument, the incidental cause or apparent cause, as contrasted with the first cause, or the ultimate cause. In the Bhagavad Gita, Krishna says, "These warriors have already been killed by me; Arjuna, you be the apparent cause (*nimitta*)" (11:33). Our effort and sadhana are the nimitta for the obstacles to be removed, but the transformation is brought about by levels of consciousness above ourselves. A seed grows into a tree; we cannot make it grow, but we can remove the impediments to its growth.

As was mentioned earlier also, it is a general lesson of all the scriptures that without God it cannot be done; but without human beings it will not be done. As Madame de Salzmann said, "Religious people talk about the Lord, *Seigneur*. That is an energy of a very high level. They say, 'The Lord helps me'. That is true. But something is required of me. I have to prepare myself for this Seigneur to help."

All our work is to prepare ourselves to be able to be useful to the Spirit. Prakriti wishes to be of service to Purusha who is seated in the heart of Prakriti. The whole purpose of Prakriti is to serve Purusha; the whole purpose of the body, or of our incarnation, is to serve the spirit. Although the body and the mind resist letting go of self-centeredness, we are deeply satisfied when there is a right relationship between the body-mind and the spirit. We need continually to return to the question about the purpose and meaning of our incarnation in this body, at this place and at this time.

Both Purusha and Prakriti are needed. The body-mind resists, but when something real is present, the body-mind gladly submits. The body-mind needs to be disciplined but not brutalized. Madame de Salzmann said, "Energies of different qualities have different durations. The energy of a higher level does not die at the death of a lower level. At the death of the body, not all the energies in the body die. These higher energies are in the body, but they are not of the body. The body is not the most important thing. The important thing is the real I, which is independent of the physical body. But the body is very necessary because the higher energy needs the body in order to manifest itself. The body is needed so that the I can have an action."

4.4

निर्माणचित्तान्यस्मितामात्रात्

nirmāṇa-chittāny-asmitā-mātrāt

Fabricating minds arise only from asmita.

4.5

प्रवृत्तिभेदे प्रयोजकं चित्तमेकमनेकेषाम्

pravṛtti-bhede prayojakaṃ chittam-ekam-anekeṣām

But there is one mind that is the source of the many minds which are involved in activity.

Asmita (I-am-this, or I-am-that) is much like *ahamkara* ("I-maker," as well as "I am the doer") in Samkhya philosophy or in the Bhagavad Gita. The question about the relationship between the One Cosmic Consciousness and individual consciousness, or between the Universal Spirit and individual soul, is extremely important. According to the sutras above, there is One Consciousness behind the various minds which are engaged in multiple activities. The sense of a separate ego arises from asmita, which according to Patañjali (2.4) is the first product of ignorance. This is what generates the separative mind fabricating this or that fantasy and ego-importance as well as fears and pervading background apprehension. It is asmita which attaches us to a small amount of consciousness, cut off from Brahman, the Vastness.

4.6

तत्र ध्यानजमनाशयम्

tatra dhyāna-jam-anāśayam

What is born of dhyana leaves no trace of impressions (*samskara*).

4.7

कर्माशुक्लाकृष्णं योगिनस्त्रिविधमितरेषाम्

karma-aśukla-akṛṣṇaṃ yoginas-trividham-itareṣām

The actions of a yogi are beyond good and evil, the actions of others are threefold (good, bad and mixed).

4.8

ततस्तद्विपाकानुगुणानामेवाभिव्यक्तिर्वासनानाम्

tatas-tad-vipāka-anuguṇānām-eva-abhivyaktir-vāsanānām

These actions sow the seeds of *vasanas*—deep tendencies and habit patterns—which bear fruit corresponding to their nature.

4.9

जातिदेशकालव्यवहितानामप्यानन्तर्यं
स्मृतिसंस्कारयोरेकरूपत्वात्

jāti-deśa-kāla-vyavahitānām-apy-ānantaryaṃ smṛti-saṃskārayor-eka-rūpatvat

Because memory and samskaras are both results of the sequence of karma, their continuity is maintained even if their cause is separated from their effect by time, by space or by lifetimes.

4.10

तासामनादित्वं चाशिषोनित्यत्वात्

tāsām anāditvaṁ cha-āśiṣo nityatvāt

These samskaras are without beginning because the desires that sustain them are everlasting.

4.11

हेतुफलाश्रयालम्बनैः संगृहीतत्वादेषामभावे तदभावः

hetu-phala-āśraya-ālambanaiḥ saṃgṛhītatvād-eṣām-abhāve tad-abhāvaḥ

Samskaras are the fruits of previous causes. When the causes are eliminated, there are no further samskaras.

The idea of *karma bandhana*, the bondage of action, is very important in Indian thought. Every action launches a series of reactions, effects, and further causes. The person initiating the action is responsible for the consequences of the action. Thus every action snares the actor in the whole web of cause and effect according to the law of karma. As was said earlier also, this law is best understood in terms of two clauses: as one is, so one acts; as one acts, so one becomes. Because of the intimate relationship between the quality of being of a person and the nature of the actions, each person's past conditions the present through the chain in which past action affects the nature of the person which in turn determines the sort of action which is likely to be done in the future. This produces the bondage of karma, slavery to the past.

The question about the kind of action which is free of the bondage of action is an important one. Krishna says in the Bhagavad Gita that all actions lead to bondage except those done as sacrifice (*yajña karma*). "Action imprisons the world unless it is done as sacrifice; freed from attachment, Arjuna, perform action as sacrifice" (3:9). Patañjali in sutra 4.6 above brings a related but different perspective: actions done in dhyana do not leave a residue. The actions of those established in dhyana are not personal; their actions are done through them rather than by them. Therefore these actions are not subject to the law of karma; they are beyond good or evil and leave no grooves or consequences, good or bad, which condition and bind. For others, actions are either good or bad or mixed and leave a residue. These residues of these actions create vasanas (habit patterns and deep tendencies) in us corresponding to the nature of the actions.

The consequences of karma, good or bad, will affect us even after many births, or even if we go a great distance away or if much time has elapsed. The working of the law of karma cannot be suspended. This is true of all the laws. None of the fundamental laws can be suspended but they can be overcome, or supplanted by higher laws. An airplane does not fly by suspending the law of gravitation, but by overcoming it with another force. Similarly, the effects of the universal law of karma can be overcome by those who have cultivated the state of dhyana.

Objective Reality

4.12

अतीतानागतं स्वरूपतोऽस्त्यध्वभेदाद्धर्माणाम्

atīta-anāgataṃ sva-rūpato' sty-adhva-bhedād-dharmāṇām

The past and the future exist within the essential form of the object, but they appear different due to the difference in the paths taken by the properties of that object.

4.13

ते व्यक्तसूक्ष्मा गुणात्मानः

te vyakta-sūkṣmā guṇa-ātmānaḥ

Manifestations of the properties, whether gross or subtle, are colored by the gunas.

4.14

परिणामैकत्वाद्वस्तुतत्त्वम्

pariṇāma-ekatvād-vastutattvam

The "thatness" (*tattvam*) of an object maintains a uniqueness through various transformations of the gunas.

4.15

वस्तुसाम्ये चित्तभेदात्तयोर्विभक्तः पन्थाः

vastusāmye chittabhedāttayorvibhaktaḥ panthāḥ

Although an object remains constant, people's perceptions of it differ because they have different associations.

4.16

न चैकचित्ततन्त्रं वस्तु तदप्रमाणकं तदा किं स्यात्

na cha-eka-chitta-tantraṁ vastu tad-apramāṇakaṃ tadā kiṃ syāt

The object is not dependent on one mind alone; otherwise, what would become of the object when not cognized by that mind?

4.17

तदुपरागापेक्षित्वाच्चित्तस्य वस्तु ज्ञाताज्ञातम्

tad-uparāga-apekṣitvāch-chittasya vastu jñāta-ajñātam

An object is known or unknown depending on whether or not a mind gets colored by it.

Time is a great mystery. Gurdjieff speaks of time as a "unique subjective." St. Augustine said, "When I am not asked about time, I know what time is. But when someone asks me about the nature of time, I do not know."

Patañjali places the sequence of time, past and future, within the object (sutra 4.12). Time itself is given an objective status as inherent to the structure of Prakriti. Because the properties of the object take through different forms (*dharmas*), we would say that change has taken place in time. What is essential to the object and what are the various forms it goes through? Water can exist as a gas, a liquid, or a solid. These different forms have different characteristics in time. But is there something which is essentially water? Patañjali answers in the affirmative: there is something about the *waterness* of the water which remains the same through all these changes. That is the *tattvam*—thatness, essential nature, suchness—of water. There is an objective reality of the object whether anyone perceives it or not. Although there is much "idealism" in Indian thought—in the philosophical sense that the perception of any object depends very heavily on the state of the cognizing mind—Patañjali, along with most of the rest of Indian philosophers, does not subscribe to an idealism in which the object depends on the cognizing mind and does not exist otherwise. For the strict idealists, such as Berkeley, an object is totally dependent for its existence on the perception of it by some mind, if not human then divine. This is not so, according to Patañjali. The essential nature or the tattvam of the object is quite unique and independent of any cognizing mind. There is an objective reality but our perception of that reality depends upon our state of consciousness. Our perception of another person or of any object or process depends upon and constitutes our relationship with that person, process, or thing.

There is an interesting story in Chhandogya Upanishad (VI.2. 1-6):

> *There was Shvetaketu Aruneya. His father said to him, "Live the life of a religious student. Verily, my dear, there is no one in our family who is unlearned, who is a Brahmana only by birth."*
>
> *He then, having become a pupil at the age of twelve, returned when he was twenty-four years of age, having studied all the Vedas, greatly conceited, thinking himself well read, arrogant. His father then said to him, "Shvetaketu, since you are now so greatly conceited, think yourself well read and arrogant, did you ask for that instruction by which the unhearable becomes heard, the unperceivable becomes perceived, the unknowable becomes known?"*
>
> *"How, Venerable Sir, can there be such teaching?"*
>
> *"Just as, my dear, by one clod of clay all that is made of clay becomes known, the modification being only a name arising from speech while the truth is that it is just clay . . . thus, my dear, is that teaching."*

When the Upanishad speaks of the various forms of clay and that all this is verily clay, the reference is to the tattvam of clay, the clayness of clay, by which all the forms of clay, the whole variety of pots made from it, can be known in their fundamental essence by someone who can bring total attention to bear on the clayness of any pot made out of clay.

Again and again, a direct perception by a purified mind is emphasized. The object exists by itself certainly; its existence does not depend on the perceiving mind, but how it is perceived depends on the quality of the perceiving mind. As long as the perceiving mind is not completely clear (or colorless) it keeps introducing blemishes in the perception of the thatness of the object.

If our mind is completely clear, it can see the real tattvam of the object. Only the chitta which is able to let Purusha reveal itself can see the true nature of Prakriti.

Mind and Spirit

4.18

सदा ज्ञाताश्चित्तवृत्तयस्तत्प्रभोः पुरुषस्यापरिणामित्वात्

sadā jñātāś-chitta-vṛttayas-tat-prabhoḥ puruṣasya-apariṇāmitvāt

Purusha, owing to its changelessness, is the master of the vrittis of chitta which it always knows.

4.19

न तत्स्वाभासं दृश्यत्वात्

na tat-sva-ābhāsaṃ dṛśyatvāt

Since chitta is an object of perception, it cannot illuminate itself.

4.20

एकसमये चोभयानवधारणम्

eka-samaye cha-ubhaya-anavadhāraṇam

Chitta cannot be aware of its object and of itself at the same time.

There are three levels: Purusha, chitta, and the objects of perception. Purusha is eternal and not subject to time; therefore it can know chitta. Chitta can be aware of the objects of perception which it can know, but chitta cannot know itself at the same time as it knows the object. Another way of saying this is that chitta's knowing power is derivative, derived from Purusha, as the light of the moon is derived from the sun. The moon is not self-luminous, nor is chitta.

4.21

चित्तान्तरदृश्ये बुद्धिबुद्धेरतिप्रसङ्गः स्मृतिसंकरश्च

chitta-antara-dṛśye buddhi-buddher-atiprasaṅgaḥ smṛti-saṃkaraś-cha

If the perception of one chitta by another chitta were postulated, there would be an endless regression of intelligence and the result would be confusion of memory.

4.22

चित्तेरप्रतिसंक्रमायास्तदाकारापत्तौ स्वबुद्धिसंवेदनम्

chitter-apratisaṃkramāyās-tad-ākāra-āpattau sva-buddhi-saṃvedanam

Chitta becomes self-aware when its consciousness assumes the immovable form of Purusha.

4.23

द्रष्टृदृश्योपरक्तं चित्तं सर्वार्थम्

draṣṭṛ-dṛśya-uparaktaṃ chittaṃ sarva-artham

Chitta which is colored both by the object and the Seer (*Purusha*) is all-apprehending.

Just as the eye cannot see itself, chitta cannot know itself. All awareness is from Purusha, the real witness or seer cannot be witnessed or seen. When chitta has the same pure form as Purusha—*sarupya* (1.4) or *samyoga* (2.17)—then it can become aware of itself. Thus what we call self-awareness is really Self-awareness, awareness not so much of the Self but by the Self.

Chitta provides experience by being colored by the objects and can lead to liberation when colored by Purusha. Again we see that chitta acts as an intermediary between Purusha and objects. But, chitta here, at this purified level, is of the nature of pure sattva, the most refined part of Prakriti. Chitta is like "psyche" (soul) in the philosophy of Plotinus: it is amphibious in character; it can sink into the matter or soar into the One. Sattva, the most refined part of the body-mind, can soar into Purusha, the One and Only Seer.

Only the chitta which is aware of both Purusha and the object, or of kshetrajña (knower of the field) as well as of kshetra (field) in the language of the Bhagavad Gita (chapter 13), is all comprehending. The real knowledge consists of both the knowledge of the field and of the knower of the field.

4.24

तदसंख्येयवासनाभिश्चित्तमपिपरार्थं संहत्यकारित्वात्

tad-asaṃkhyeya-vāsanābhiś-chittam-api para-arthaṃ saṃhatya-kāritvāt

And chitta, despite its countless habits, exists for the sake of the Other (*Purusha*) on whom it is dependent.

4.25

विशेषदर्शिन आत्मभावभावना विनिवृत्तिः

viśeṣa-darśina ātma-bhāva-bhāvanā-vinivṛttiḥ

One who sees the distinction between the mind and Atman ceases to cultivate the self.

4.26

तदा विवेकनिम्नं कैवल्यप्राग्भारं चित्तम्

tadā viveka-nimnaṃ kaivalya-prāgbhāraṃ chittam

Then, deep in viveka, chitta gravitates towards Kaivalya.

Again and again, Patañjali returns to the question of the purpose of Prakriti or of incarnation, and here in the particular form of chitta. "Why do you have a body?" asked Madame de Salzmann. This question could equally well be expressed as "Why do you have a mind?" Or "Why do you exist?" For Patañjali the answer is unequivocal: everything in Prakriti exists for the purposes of Purusha; Prakriti has no purposes of its own. As Madame de Salzmann said, "The body must serve something else. It cannot serve itself, for it is designed for destruction."

The Spirit needs the body in order to know itself. Purified chitta becomes a spotless mirror in which Purusha can see its own true form.

"There is an energy which is trying to evolve. That is why it comes into a body. If a person works and helps the evolution of this energy, at death this energy goes to a higher level. If one does not work, the energy returns to its own level. But the human life is wasted," said Madame de Salzmann. The whole raison d'être of the human incarnation is for the sake of the subtler energy which for its own purposes needs a body and comes into a body.

The whole of the Indian tradition is quite unequivocal in saying that the Spirit (Atman, Purusha) is above the mind (chitta), and that the real knower is not the mind, but Purusha which knows through the mind. Besides, as the sutra 4.25 above says, when one is completely clear about the distinction between Purusha and chitta, then one is freed of all sense of egoism, asmita, I-ness.

In contrast to all spiritual traditions, Descartes explicitly maintained that "spirit" is the same as "soul" and that "soul" is the same as "mind," all belonging to the realm of *res cogitans* (thinking beings) as contrasted with the whole of nature, including the body and the animals, which belongs to *res extensa* (physical world). This resulted in the mind-body, or in theological terms soul-body dualism. In the Cartesian system, which has had an enormous effect on Western philosophy and theology, there is not a place for the transformable chitta (mind, soul) which can be purified by spiritual practice and can provide a dynamic link between Purusha and Prakriti by becoming aware of the distinction between the two.

Madame de Salzmann said, "What religions call God is the higher level, above the mind, but understood through a higher part of the mind. Man is made to create a link between two levels, to receive energy from a higher level in order to have an action on the level below—not a reaction."

Each one of us has a subjective reality, determined by the conditioning—of our species, of our culture, gender, religion, family, personal history in this life and in our previous lives. To be free or liberated is to be free of our past and of conditioning. Liberation (*Moksha*, *Mukti*, *Nirvana*, *Kaivalya*) is freedom from the tyranny of time. We see repeatedly that true freedom is freedom not for myself but from myself. Real freedom is not a license to do what the ego likes; a free person naturally conforms to the cosmic laws. Unified internally, such a person's wishes, desires, intentions and undertakings are indivisible. A sage voluntarily places the ego-self under the laws of higher being, of Purusha. Madame de Salzmann said, "True individuality consists in voluntarily placing oneself under a law."

When chitta has developed viveka, that is, when the mind has developed discernment, it naturally gravitates towards Kaivalya, unconditioned freedom, the aloneness of the power of seeing. At the highest level, a difference between Purusha and the most refined part of chitta cannot be identified. When Chitta is one with Purusha, Purusha has found a bride in Prakriti, and there is ecstasy of union.

Freedom Without Measure

4.27

तच्छिद्रेषु प्रत्ययान्तराणिसंस्कारेभ्यः

tach-chhidreṣu pratyaya-antarāṇi saṃskārebhyaḥ

In the process of chitta gravitating to Kaivalya, interruptions may arise due to past samskaras.

4.28

हानमेषां क्लेशवदुक्तम्

hānam-eṣāṃ kleśavad-uktam

They can be removed in the same manner as the kleshas.

4.29

प्रसंख्यानेऽप्यकुसीदस्य सर्वथा विवेकख्यातेर्धर्ममेघः समाधिः

prasaṃkhyāne' py-akusīdasya sarvathā viveka-khyāter-dharma-meghaḥ samādhiḥ

One who, due to perfect discrimination, is totally non-grasping even of the highest rewards, remains in constant viveka, which is called *dharmamegha* (cloud of dharma) samadhi.

4.30

ततः क्लेशकर्मनिवृत्तिः

tataḥ kleśa-karma-nivṛttiḥ

From that follows freedom from action colored by kleshas.

4.31

तदा सर्वावरणमलापेतस्य ज्ञानस्यानन्त्याज्ज्ञेयमल्पम्

tadā sarva-āvaraṇa-mala-apetasya jñānasya-ānantyāj-jñeyam-alpam

Then all the coverings and impurities of knowledge are totally removed. Because of the vastness of this jñana, little remains to be known.

Even when almost the entire ground of consciousness has been cleansed, there may still be distractions. Other inclinations, taking us away from Purusha, may arise because of previous samskaras (subliminal impressions), from childhood or from previous lives. As long as we are alive, there will be a pull towards self-occupation. The effort to be free of self-occupation needs to be undertaken again and again. The task is difficult because we exist at every level of Prakriti, and the world is full of many distractions, interesting projects, temptations, and fears.

The process described for the attenuation of the hindrances or the kleshas, (in sutras 2.10-11), is pratiprasava—a reversal of the flow of the usual tendencies of the mind, a metanoia, turning inwards rather than the natural tendency of turning outwards. This leads to a subtler and quieter level of consciousness and a steadiness of attention.

Patañjali had earlier (1.16) said that the higher form of detachment, of vairagya, results from a vision of Purusha or Self. Here, being situated in the discerning vision of Purusha, with vairagya towards even the highest rewards, there is dharmamegha (literally, a cloud of dharma) samadhi. This expression may have been borrowed from the Mahayana Buddhist literature in which it occurs frequently. However, dharmamegha is like saying "ritambhara tatra prajña" (there the insight is naturally full of order) as in 1.48. The suggestion is that at this stage, the aspirant is enveloped in a cloud of order and truth. It is a cloud of unknowing—because we cannot know Purusha or God, but with a steady vision of discernment without distractions, or an unwavering love as described in the great Christian spiritual classic, *The Cloud of Unknowing*, it is possible to be lifted into that cloud and to be embraced by Purusha.

This is the stage of the "beloved" in meditation, as briefly described earlier. The god Krishna pines for and embraces Radha, the archetypical representation of the human soul, as delicately described in the great love poem *Gita Govinda* of Jayadeva.

There is an interesting distinction between the Indic approach which ultimately takes its stand either on love (*bhakti*) or on viveka and the Christian approach which takes its stand largely on love. The emphasis on viveka is much more masculine, whereas the emphasis on love is much more feminine. Many of the great warriors of the spirit in India—Yajñavalkya, Patañjali, Mahavira, the Buddha, Shankara—are *arahatas* (Pali for the Sanskrit *arihantas* meaning "killers of the enemies"), *nirgrantha* (without knots or scriptures), *maharathi* (great charioteers), and the like. They do not surrender; they almost seem to conquer.

In a different mode, the Bhakti saints like Mira, Surdas, and Tulsi surrender themselves to the spirit, yearning to be the beloved of God. Jayadeva tells the story of the love between the god Krishna and Radha, the human soul, between Purusha and Prakriti. Radha pines for union with Krishna, but Krishna also pines for union with Radha. The poet, Jayadeva, in his sadhana came to the stage of becoming the beloved himself. He is delighted with Krishna, and is wholly receptive; all action now belongs to Krishna, not to Jayadeva. Jayadeva could not write the final scene in which Krishna and Radha, the beloved, are united in love. Legend has it that Krishna himself came and wrote the final scene in which Radha rides Krishna in a passionate and joyous play of love. Jayadeva did not, and could not, initiate any action, even that of completing his poem; it is all up to Krishna.[1]

It is interesting to note that all the commandments of Christ, given in general—"Love God," "Love thy neighbor as thyself"—or specifically to the disciples—"Love each other as I have loved you," "Love your enemies"—have the word "love" in them. In the Indic philosophic thought, as indeed in the practical teaching of Christ himself, strictly speaking we cannot love God, but we can be loved by God. Whenever disciples say, "Lord, I love you," Christ stops them and says, "If any one loves me, he will keep my word. Then my Father will love him, and we shall come to him and abide in him" (John 14:23). If the disciples remain rightly ordered internally, which is to say that they abide in Christ, and Christ abides in them through his words and love, then they are connected with the Source of all energy. Then they are one with the Vastness, within which they are hierarchically ordered, and they are able to accomplish everything they will, precisely because what they will is not to do their own personal projects but to do that alone which is in harmony with the will of the Source. Christ himself is the model: he loves his disciples as his Father loves him; he obeys the Father, as they must obey him. This is how he dwells in the Father's love, as they must dwell in his. "And you will dwell in my love if you keep my commandments, just as I have kept my Father's commandments and dwell in His love"(John 15:10).

We should not over emphasize the difference in the approaches focused on love and on viveka. They are both needed. With so many sages in India—especially with Kabir, Ramakrishna, and Vivekananda—bhakti and viveka very much come together in the higher levels of consciousness. We see a strong emphasis on viveka in *The Cloud of Unknowing* in keeping a clear distinction between what is God—although unknowable and therefore in and above the cloud of unknowing—and what is not God and therefore to be placed in the cloud of forgetting. "Just as the *cloud of unknowing* lies above you, between you and your God, so you must fashion a *cloud of forgetting* beneath you, between you and every created thing." (*The Cloud of Unknowing*, p. 53)

The only thing which is needed is to remember that God, or Purusha or Brahman, exists, and that we exist under His gaze. The only practice that is needed is the practice of the remembrance of the presence of God. Everything else follows from that one thing. A natural consequence of the dharmamegha samadhi is a freedom from kleshas and karma bandhana. All the obstacles to real jñana, gnosis, are destroyed when we dwell in the Spirit or in Purusha. Then nothing that matters is left to be known.

4.32

ततः कृतार्थानां परिणामक्रमसमाप्तिर्गुणानाम्

tataḥ kṛta-arthānaṃ pariṇāma-krama-samāptir-guṇānām

Then the sequence of transformations (*parinama*) of the gunas ends, because they have fulfilled their purpose.

4.33

क्षणप्रतियोगी परिणामापरान्तनिर्ग्राह्यः क्रमः

kṣaṇa-pratiyogī pariṇāma-apara-anta-nirgrāhyaḥ kramaḥ

Time succession and its correlates, moments in time, are ended with the ending of parinama.

The body-mind or the individualized Prakriti which functions through the gunas has now fulfilled its purpose. The yogi is freed from the constraints of the body as well as of all materiality, including space and time. As the transformations of the gunas end, the succession in time, sequence, ends, and the aspirant's consciousness rests in a dimension freed of time. As it is said in the case of the Buddha after his enlightenment, one who is established in yoga becomes *kala vimukta* (freed from time, timeless, eternal) as well as *trikala darshi* (seer of three times—past, present, and future).

A periodic reminder is needed: to be free of the body does not mean to be rid of the body. The spiritual journey is not possible without the body. Everything takes place in the body, and the body is very important, but it is not the ultimate thing. Here is a remark of Madame de Salzmann:

> *The body is necessary, but it is not the most important thing. It must obey something else. In fact, the body wants and likes the contact with the energy which comes from above, which comes from God. But we are taken by automatism. One must liberate the subtle body from the prison of habits of the ordinary body. The important thing is the real*

I, which is independent of the physical body. But the body is very necessary because the higher energy needs the body in order to manifest itself. The body is needed so that the I can have an action. That I can create a new body if the connection is strong enough, that is to say, if one permits the higher energy to pass into me. The conscious response or attention, which arises from the me, which is personal, serves as a thread for connecting the I and the me. The I is not personal. I can awaken me and serve the Earth. The Earth as a whole has need of more conscious energy.

4.34

पुरुषार्थशून्यानां गुणानां प्रतिप्रसवः कैवल्यं स्वरूपप्रतिष्ठा वा चितिशक्तिरिति

puruṣa-artha-śūnyānāṃ guṇānāṃ pratiprasavaḥ kaivalyaṃ sva-rūpa-pratiṣṭhā vā chiti-śaktir-iti

The gunas, their purpose fulfilled, return to their original state and pure unbounded Purusha remains forever established in its essential nature. This is Kaivalya, freedom without measure, the Aloneness of the power of seeing. It is thus.

When the gunas, the constituents and the forces of Prakriti, have fulfilled their purpose in this way, no further transformation is necessary or possible. All the elements of Prakriti return to their state of original harmony, and the pure Unbounded Purusha is eternally established in its own absolute and essential nature. This brings us back to what was already mentioned in the beginning of the *Yoga Sutras* (1.3).

Kaivalya is the state of Aloneness: freedom without measure and the power of pure seeing. This is not a state of isolation of Purusha from Prakriti, as is unfortunately sometimes maintained by translators and commentators, but the state in which the seer, the seen and seeing are one. In the happy phrase of Plotinus, this is the "flight of the alone to the Alone."

This is Self-realization, making the Self real in actuality. Now one has become truly what one always was and is. We could say that now the searcher knows the answer to the quest "Who am I?" It is better to say that now the whole body-mind and the entire life of the searcher lives the answer to this question.

The question "*Koham*? Who am I?" is responded with "*Soham*. I AM." And there is ananda, celebration and joy, without measure.

Endnotes:

1 *Gita Govinda* is a classic of mystical love and has had a large impact on the culture of India—especially in poetry, painting, dance, and music. There has been an unbroken recitation every day from this book in a great temple in Orissa for nearly eight hundred years.

May We All Be Blessed into Usefulness

The real obstacle on any spiritual path is the passivity of attention, in our own lives and towards our lives. Without an active attention we cannot take responsibility for our life. This passivity is cosmological in nature and arises owing to the inherent dynamism of Prakriti with its outward tendencies. Everything, both what we find pleasant and what we find unpleasant, happens mechanically according to the laws of nature inside us as well as outside, and will continue in this way. If we do not bring an active attention, we are only objects affected by the play of forces. If we do bring active attention, the forces still operate, but as we become more and more aware of them we can participate in the vast play of Prakriti with more consciousness.

A dependence on traditions, scriptures, gurus, social customs or scholars and theologians or upon the approval of others leads to a fear of disapproval, and a need to maintain the status quo, abhinivesha. The obverse side of fear is pretension and a need for self-assertion, which leads to the self-importance of asmita. Thus, self-doubt is the source of self-importance. A need for approval lies behind all efforts of evangelism. If someone else can be convinced, that will show us that we are on the right path. The attempt to convince someone of anything is a mark of insecurity.

The kleshas of abhinivesha and asmita, which lead to fear and self-importance are maintained in the darkness of ignorance, but when we look, when we become conscious of our situation, we see that we are not what we might be. We find ourselves living in a haze of non-awareness, as if asleep, veiled from reality, constantly reacting to external events and actions; we see that we are not free. Conditioned by the past, we find ourselves unable to respond freshly to situations and people. Then a subtle yearning expresses itself in us: we wish to wake up to the real, to be mindfully aware of the present situation and to respond with freedom.

In spiritual matters, a certain amount of restlessness or dissatisfaction, or hunger, is an indication that something is still alive in us and that we still wish for something other than what we now are. There is a classical expression in the Rig Veda, "*neti*, *neti*," which means "not yet, not yet." It is an indication of an ongoing search. Whenever we are satisfied, we are no longer searching.

The main source of this dissatisfaction is the awareness in us of the gap between what we know and what we are. We often know what the right thing to do is, what the right dharma, responsibility, is; but we find ourselves unable to carry it out. This is why yoga is needed—so that we can learn to be disciplined, learn to cultivate steadier and steadier attention, and learn to search for the essential. In a conversation with Madame de Salzmann I once told her about a recurring feeling that I live as if the whole cosmos was designed for my benefit, for me to get ahead. She said, "This is why one needs to work. To have a different relation with the world. Human beings are links between two levels. One needs to learn to work consciously in order to pay for one's existence."

The more developed and the steadier our attention is, the closer we are to Purusha, which is pure seeing, or pure attention. The more active our attention is, the higher we are on the axis of Purusha. Purusha is not an object of attention; in that sense it cannot be passive. The only appropriate grammatical case applicable to Purusha is third person singular nominative. The more the passivity, the closer to dead matter we are. A feature of passivity is predictability, subjection to laws and bondage. The closer something is to dead matter at absolute zero temperature, the more predictable it is. The closer it is to the Spirit or God or Purusha, the less predictable it is. The Spirit bloweth where it listeth, as is said in the Bible. The ability to surprise oneself or to surprise another and also to be surprised is a mark of freedom.

Patañjali recommends abhyasa, vairagya and Ishvara pranidhana as the main practices, all under the overarching canopy of viveka so that we would acquire finer and finer attention and a corresponding discernment in order to distinguish between the Real and the relatively less real. With a more conscious awareness of the situation and a more developed conscience, we can participate more and more in the Real. Spiritual development is a cosmological need; it is not only the need of an individual undertaking a spiritual discipline. It is important for the establishment and the maintenance of true order that there be the right relationship between Purusha and Prakriti, between the Spirit and the body. Then there can be the right flow of subtle energies from above downwards. Otherwise, Prakriti itself falls into chaos—and by the principle of analogy, our planet and our body will fall into sickness and disease.

The function and purpose of a human being is to become a link, a conduit, for Purusha to manifest through Prakriti, for higher energy to come down to the Earth—to bring Heaven down to Earth. Our Father who is in Heaven may do His will here on Earth as He does in Heaven, but this is possible only if the River Ganga which flows in Heaven may flow down to the Earth, the body, and irrigate her. The Rig Veda says we are children of Heaven and of Earth. Perhaps we have forgotten our connection with Heaven. Letting this energy descend into the body is to let Heaven come down to Earth. That is the incarnation of the Word. Again quoting Meister Eckhart: "Every Christian is called to be Mary and give birth to the Word."

In general, we do not see what the life of the Earth is; nor do we see what our responsibility is in the maintenance and evolution of the life of the Earth. But a part of us understands. It is necessary that the connection with the conscious energy be strengthened. When we undertake a sustained spiritual effort, as in yoga, a fine energy comes from above and has an effect on the whole body, and by osmosis on the Earth. This requires a very strong and steady effort. We must work for ourselves and for the Earth. In this way, we can approach the great Bodhisattva vow to help the evolution of all sentient beings.

The emphasis on abhyasa assumes that there is a process, and some progress can be made by persistence in practice. Abhyasa requires determination, persistence in inquiry, and steadfastness in effort. There is a *doha* of Saint Kabir:

> *Karat karat abhyasa se, jadamati bhaye sujan.*
> *Rasri avat jata se sil par pare nishan.*
>
> *By repeated abhyasa, even a dull mind*
> *becomes a knower.*
> *By the repeated movement of the rope*
> *even a hard rock gets marked.*

Real vairagya is not a renunciation of this or that, but it is a renunciation of that in me who is addicted to myself as I am. It is freedom from myself, from selfishness; it is a non-identification with myself, with my sufferings and pleasures, with my fears and desires, with my knowledge and experiences. It is really a dying to myself so that a radically new being can be born in me. Vairagya is the essential quality for placing everything under the cloud of forgetting so that we can be turned more and more towards the cloud of unknowing. We do not know Purusha, we cannot know Purusha, but we can be more and more drawn to it. Love is at the heart of vairagya. We can be more easily detached from something if we are attached to something superior in quality. This is why Patañjali says that "The higher vairagya arises from a vision of the Transcendent Being (*Purusha*) and leads to the cessation of craving for the things of the world" (1.16). There are two ways of non-identification: one is the result of a recognition of the negative effects of craving, of being snared in the nets of the world. The other is the higher and it is a result of a glimpse of the kingdom of heaven, of the higher possibility, a vision of God, even a fleeting awareness of Purusha.

Ishvara pranidhana, the love for God or for Purusha is the real motivation for vairagya. This then also expresses itself as love for the uniqueness of everything in nature and for the world generally. This love is not pity, but love for the life within every creature, and therefore a wish to serve. A dedication to service is not for the sake of the others, but because the Creator is seated in the heart of every creature. Krishna repeatedly declares in the Bhagavad Gita that he is seated in the heart of everyone. In a television interview with Mother Teresa, an interviewer once said, "You must love the poor." He was not at all prepared for her answer, "No, I don't love the poor." The interviewer was thoroughly flummoxed by this. After some hesitation, he said, "But you spend so much time and energy taking care of the poor and the sick. You must love them." She said, "I don't love the poor; I love the Christ in them."

Vivekananda, the extraordinary late nineteenth century sage of India, said, "For thy good, O Shraman, may thine be Vairagya, the feeling of which is love, which unifies all inequalities, cures the disease of Samsara, removes the three-fold misery inevitable in the phenomenal world, reveals the true nature of all things, destroys the darkness of Maya, and which brings out the Selfhood of everything from Brahma to the blade of grass!" (Badrinath, p. 352).

What Vivekananda here is calling Selfhood of everything is uniqueness or individuality in a true sense. This uniqueness is a manifestation of the essential Oneness of all there is.

Ishvara pranidhana is a celebration of the Mystery that cannot be known. The surrender to God is really surrendering to what is the deepest within ourselves, rather than to what is superficial in us. It is a recognition of the higher dimensions, of worlds within worlds. In a state of wonder we are no longer convinced that we know all there is to know. Wonder requires a state of unknowing—not a state of ignorance, but of innocence in which one is free from knowledge, known, knower and the need to know. Then sometimes one is connected with a quality of awareness in which the Mystery is still not solved, and it has no publicly communicable logical answer, but it is dissolved. This Mystery no longer troubles one or makes one apprehensive or anxious; it does not evoke a denial or a rejection. The only response to it is celebration—in dance or music or painting or science or philosophy or love.

At the heart of all practice in the *Yoga Sutras* is viveka. Real viveka is to distinguish between what belongs to the cloud of forgetting and what belongs to the cloud of unknowing, discernment between Purusha and not-Purusha. Towards one a searcher will cultivate vairagya, towards the other a dedication and submission.

The inevitable consequences of all practice are both wisdom and compassion, better to say love, which is love of God and love for the creatures of God. We become responsible for the welfare of and the maintenance of order in the creation—on the planet, in the society, in the family, and in ourselves—as we begin to see that it is God manifesting Himself in His creation and we are instruments of His care for the world.

"The last, and the highest manifestation of Prana (life force) is love. The moment you have succeeded in manufacturing love out of Prana, you are free. It is the hardest and the greatest thing to gain."—Vivekananda (Badrinath, p. 307).

"All expansion is life, all contraction is death. All love is expansion, all selfishness is contraction. Love is therefore the only law of life. He who loves lives, he who is selfish is dying. Therefore, love for love's sake, because it is the only law of life, just as you breathe to live. This is the secret of selfless love, selfless action, and the rest."—Vivekananda (Badrinath, p. vi).

There is always a wonder, even awe, connected with an encounter with Mystery. "Unless it is wonderful, wonderful, it cannot be holy," says an Upanishad. There is a non-canonical saying of Jesus Christ, found on some papyri discovered in Oxyrhynchus in Egypt at the end of the nineteenth century: "Let not him who seeks cease until he finds, and when he finds he shall be astonished. Astonished he shall reach the Kingdom, and having reached the Kingdom, he shall rest."

But until then, we listen to Rainer Maria Rilke:

> *. . . Be patient towards all that's unsolved in your heart*
> *And learn to love the questions themselves.*
> *Like locked rooms*
> *and like books that are written in a foreign tongue*
>
> *Do not seek the answers that cannot be given to you,*
> *because you would not be able to live them.*

And the point is to live everything.

Live the questions now.
Perhaps you will then, gradually, without noticing it.
Live along some distant day into the answers.

—Letter 3, *Letters to a Young Poet*

To hold a question about the meaning and purpose of life is a quest, a journey without end. A questioning which demands answers becomes an inquisition. Settling for doctrines or formulations kills the inquiry.

The middle path is not a middling path; there is no refuge in the security of one doctrine or another. It is as sharp as a razor's edge, as the Katha Upanishad says, and calls for me to live in inquiry, not knowing but wondering. Who am I? Why am I here?

I am in question and I am the question, but it is not for myself. It is for the sake of Purusha, the Wholly Other, Unknown and Mysterious. It is a wonder that the Wholly Other is intimately myself. And there is a celebration of this Mystery.

May we all be blessed into willingness and usefulness!

The Yoga Sutras in Translation

Timeless Insight

1.1

Here, now, is the teaching of yoga.

1.2

Yoga is establishing the mind (*chitta*) in stillness.

1.3

Then the Seer dwells in its essential nature.

1.4

Otherwise the movements of the mind (*vrittis*) are regarded as the Seer.

1.5

There are five types of vrittis, which may be pleasant or unpleasant.

1.6

These are true knowledge, false knowledge, imagination, sleep, and memory.

1.7

True knowledge is based upon perception, inference, and valid testimony.

1.8
False knowledge is conception with no basis in reality.

1.9
Imagination is thought based on images conjured up by words devoid of substance.

1.10
Sleep depends upon and leads to non-being.

1.11
Memory is recollecting past experience.

1.12
Stillness develops through practice (*abhyasa*) and non-identification (*vairagya*).

1.13
Abhyasa is the effort of remaining present.

1.14
Continuous care and attention for a long time establishes this practice.

1.15
Vairagya is the mastery over the craving for what has been seen or heard.

1.16
The higher vairagya arises from a vision of the Transcendent Being (*Purusha*) and leads to the cessation of craving for the things of the world.

1.17
Samprajñata is the state of consciousness in which there is an awareness of the object with thought, reflection, pleasure and a sense of a separate self (*asmita*).

1.18

Beyond this, when the mind is emptied with practice, there is a state in which only the trace impressions (*samskaras*) remain.

1.19

This is the nature of existence for beings without physical bodies and for those who are absorbed in the womb of life awaiting reincarnation.

1.20

For others, this state is realized through faith, will, mindfulness, tranquility, and wisdom.

1.21

It is near for those who ardently desire it.

1.22

Even among these there are degrees—mild, moderate, and intense.

1.23

Samadhi—timeless insight and integration—may be reached by self-surrender to God (Ishvara).

1.24

Free of the bondage of action, the laws of cause and effect, and past impressions, Ishvara is the unique being who is unaffected by suffering.

1.25

In Ishvara lies the incomparable seed of all insight and wisdom.

1.26

Unconditioned by time, Ishvara is also the teacher of earlier seers.

1.27

Om is the expression of Ishvara.

1.28

Repetition of this sacred syllable can lead to the realization of its meaning.

1.29

Then there is no interference and inward-mindedness is attained.

1.30

Sickness, apathy, doubt, carelessness, laziness, indulgence, confusion, unsteadiness, and feeling stuck are the interruptions which cause dispersion of attention.

1.31

Dissatisfaction, despair, nervousness, and irregular breathing accompany this dispersion.

1.32

Dispersion is prevented by the practice of focusing on one truth (*tattva*).

1.33

A clear and tranquil mind results from cultivating friendliness towards those who are happy, compassion towards those who suffer, joy towards the virtuous, and impartiality towards wrong-doers.

1.34

Or from attention to the outward and inward flow of breath (*prana*).

1.35

Or from steady attention to subtler levels of sensation.

1.36

Or by experiencing inner radiance free from sorrow.

1.37

Or by turning to those things which do not incite attachment.

1.38

Or by depending upon insights obtained in the states of greater awakening called *svapna* and *nidra*.

1.39

Or by meditating on the longing of the heart.

1.40

For one whose mind is clear, mastery extends from the most minute particle to the largest expanse.

1.41

When the vrittis are diminished, the mind is like a clear diamond which reflects what is before it. Then fusion (*samapatti*) of perceiver, perceiving, and the object of perception takes place.

1.42

Savitarka samapatti is knowledge (*jñana*) based on thought, words and their meaning.

1.43

Nirvitarka samapatti is knowledge beyond thought, when memory is purified, emptied of its subjectivity, and the object alone shines forth.

1.44

Similarly, subtler savichara samapatti (fusion) involving reflection and nirvichara samapatti, beyond reflection, are also explained.

1.45

The range of subtle objects includes all levels of creation, extending to the limits of the unmanifest.

1.46

These four levels of samapatti refer to samadhi seeded by external objects (*sabija samadhi*).

1.47

Further refinement of nirvichara brings lucidity of the authentic self.

1.48

There, insight is full of order.

1.49

The knowledge obtained in this state of consciousness is different from the knowledge obtained by testimony or by inference because of its distinct purpose.

1.50

The subtle samskaras produced by this knowledge prevent the further accumulation of other impressions.

1.51

When even the subtle samskaras have subsided, all movement of the mind ceases and there is contemplation without seed (*nirbija samadhi*).

Practice

2.1

The practice of yoga consists of self-discipline (*tapas*), self-study (svad-hyaya), and dedication to Ishvara.

2.2

Yoga is for cultivating samadhi and for weakening the hindrances (*kleshas*).

2.3

The kleshas are ignorance (*avidya*), the sense of a separate self (*asmita*), attraction (*raga*), aversion (*dvesha*), and clinging to the status quo (*abhinivesha*).

2.4

Avidya is the cause of all the others, whether dormant, attenuated, intermittent, or fully active.

2.5

Avidya is seeing the transient as eternal, the impure as pure, dissatisfaction as pleasure, the non-Self as Self.

2.6
Asmita is the misidentification of the power of seeing with what is seen.

2.7
Raga arises from dwelling on pleasant experiences.

2.8
Dvesha arises from clinging to unpleasant experiences.

2.9
Abhinivesha is the automatic tendency for continuity; it overwhelms even the wise.

2.10
These subtle kleshas can be overcome by reversing the natural flow (pratiprasava) and returning to the source.

2.11
Their effects can be reduced by meditation (*dhyana*).

2.12
Past actions, rooted in kleshas, give rise to experiences in present or future births.

2.13
As long as the root exists, the effects will be experienced as birth and in the quality and duration of life.

2.14
Joy is the result of right action, sorrow of wrong action.

2.15
For the discerning, all is sorrow, resulting from the mismatch between what is actual and what is thought, and because of the suffering inherent in change, pain, and from past conditioning.

2.16
Future suffering is to be avoided.

2.17
The cause of suffering is the misidentification of the seer with the seen.

2.18
The seen consists of material elements and the sense organs. These have qualities of clarity, activity, and stability. The seen exists to serve the aims of experience and liberation.

2.19
Everything that exists, whether particular, general, manifest, or unmanifest is constituted by the gunas, the fundamental qualities of nature.

2.20
The Seer is only the power of pure seeing. Although pure, the Seer appears to see with the mind.

2.21
The seen is for the sake of the Seer.

2.22
Having served its purpose, for one who is liberated, the phenomenal world no longer appears as before, but it continues as such for others.

2.23
The connection between the Seer and the seen causes a mistaken perception of identity between the force of the visible and the power to see.

2.24
The cause of this is ignorance (*avidya*).

2.25
With the disappearance of ignorance, the misidentification no longer exists. Then pure seeing alone remains.

2.26
Steady vision of discernment (*viveka*) is the way to overcome ignorance.

2.27
Wisdom (*prajña*) is accomplished in seven stages.

2.28
By practicing the limbs of yoga, impurity is destroyed and the radiance of jñana leads to viveka.

2.29
The eight limbs of yoga are: yama (self-restraint), niyama (right observance), asana (right alignment or posture), pranayama (regulation of breath), pratyahara (withdrawal of the senses), dharana (concentration), dhyana (meditation), and samadhi (free attention).

2.30
The yamas are non-violation, truthfulness, non-stealing, containment, and non-grasping.

2.31
These restraints are not limited by birth, time, or circumstance; they constitute the great vow everywhere.

2.32
The niyamas are purity, contentment, self-discipline (*tapas*), self-study (*svadhyaya*), and dedication to Ishvara.

2.33
When negative thoughts and feelings arise, the opposite should be cultivated.

2.34
Cultivating the opposite is realizing that negative feelings, such as that of violence, result in endless suffering and ignorance—whether these feelings are acted out, instigated or condoned, whether motivated by greed, anger, or delusion, whether these are mild, medium, or extreme.

2.35
In the presence of one who is established in ahimsa, there is cessation of hostility.

2.36
When one abides in truthfulness, actions result in their desired end.

2.37
When one is established in non-stealing, riches present themselves freely.

2.38
When brahmacharya is established, great vigor is obtained.

2.39
When one is established in non-grasping, there is knowledge of the nature and purpose of existence.

2.40
Purity leads to non-identification with one's own body and to a freedom from the need for contact with others.

2.41
Purity of mind, cheerfulness, mastery of the senses, one-pointedness, and ability for Self-realization follow.

2.42
Contentment leads to unsurpassed joy.

2.43
Self-discipline leads to the destruction of impurity and to the perfection of the body and the senses.

2.44
From self-study one reaches union with the chosen deity (ishta devata).

2.45
Perfection in samadhi arises from dedication to Ishvara.

2.46
Right alignment (asana) is accompanied by steadiness and ease.

2.47
This is attained when there is complete relaxation and samapatti (fusion, union) with the Infinite.

2.48

Then one is no longer assailed by opposing dualities.

2.49

With right alignment, the regulation of the flow of breath in and out is pranayama.

2.50

When the movement of breath in and out and the stopping of breath are observed, according to time, place, and number, breathing becomes deep and subtle.

2.51

The fourth stage of pranayama takes one beyond the domain of inner and outer.

2.52

Then the covering over the inner light of truth is dissolved.

2.53

And the mind (*manas*) becomes fit for dharana.

2.54

Pratyahara is the withdrawal of the senses from their objects by following the essential nature of the mind.

2.55

From this comes the perfect mastery over the senses.

The Way of Splendor

3.1

Dharana is holding the mind in one place.

3.2

Dhyana is the uninterrupted flow of awareness towards the object of attention.

3.3
Samadhi is the state when the self is not, when there is awareness only of the object of meditation.

3.4
Total attention (*samyama*) is when dharana, dhyana, and samadhi are together.

3.5
The illumination of insight results from the mastery of this.

3.6
The practice of samyama is accomplished gradually.

3.7
These three limbs of yoga are inner limbs with respect to the limbs discussed previously.

3.8
Still, these are external to nirbija samadhi.

3.9
Nirodha parinama, the transformation towards silence, is the transformation of the mind in which the attention moves from the rise and fall of the external impressions to the silence which pervades when the mind is settled.

3.10
The flow of silence becomes constant from the internal impressions of this quiet.

3.11
Samadhi parinama, the transformation towards realization, is the gradual settling of distractions and the simultaneous rising of one-pointedness.

3.12
Ekagrata parinama, the transformation towards one-pointedness, is the

stage of transformation in which activity and silence are equally balanced in the mind.

3.13

By extension, the transformations of the mind explain the transformations of material nature—transformations of quality, form, and state.

3.14

The substratum underlying the essential properties of material nature endures whether these properties are at rest, arising, or unmanifest.

3.15

Variations in the sequence of properties cause differences in the transformation of material nature.

3.16

By samyama on the three kinds of transformations (*nirodha*, *samadhi*, *ekagrata*) knowledge of the past and of the future can be gained.

3.17

Understanding of an object is usually confused because the name, the meaning, and the perception of the object are mistakenly identified. Through samyama on the distinction among these three, the knowledge of the sound of all beings can be gained.

3.18

Knowledge of previous births can be gained from direct perception of samskaras.

3.19

Through direct perception of their intention, knowledge of another's mind can be gained.

3.20

This does not involve knowledge of the underlying object of thought since that is not in one's field of perception.

3.21

From samyama on the form of the body, by breaking the contact between the eye of the observer and the light reflected by the body, the body becomes invisible.

3.22

From samyama on the immediate and remote effects of action (karma) foreknowledge of death can be gained.

3.23

From samyama on friendliness and similar qualities, these qualities can be gained.

3.24

From samyama on the strength of an animal, such as an elephant, one gains that strength.

3.25

Knowledge of the subtle, the concealed and the remote can be achieved by directing the inner light.

3.26

Knowledge of the universe can be gained by samyama on the sun.

3.27

Knowledge of the arrangement of the stars can be gained by samyama on the moon.

3.28

Knowledge of the movement of the stars can be gained by samyama on the polar star.

3.29

Knowledge of the bodily system can be gained by samyama on the navel center.

3.30

Hunger and thirst can be overcome by samyama on the throat hollow.

3.31

Stability can be achieved by samyama on the kurma nadi (tortoise vein).

3.32

Samyama on the light in the head brings vision of perfected beings.

3.33

And, knowledge of the all can be reached through intuitive perception.

3.34

Samyama on the heart leads to an understanding of chitta.

3.35

When the quality of perfect sattva is close to the quality of Purusha, experience serves Purusha. By samyama on the purposes of perfect sattva, one gains insight into Purusha.

3.36

Thus, subtle hearing, touching, seeing, tasting, and smelling are born.

3.37

These powers (*siddhis*) are attainments in the world, but they are impediments to samadhi.

3.38

Being free of the sources of bondage, perceiving the manifestations of another, one is able to enter their body through consciousness.

3.39

From the mastery of the movement of subtle breath rising in the body, one is freed from being caught by mud, thorns, and water, and one can rise above them.

3.40

Radiance is the result of mastery of the movement of the mid-breath.

3.41

The divine ear develops with samyama on the connection between ear and space.

3.42

From samyama on the connection between the body and space and by samapatti with the lightness of cotton, one can move through space at will.

3.43

The veil covering the light within is destroyed by contacting the state of consciousness which is beyond the body and is inconceivable.

3.44

From samyama on gross, intrinsic, subtle, relational, and purposive aspects of the elements of matter, one attains mastery over them.

3.45

Then extraordinary powers appear, such as the power to be as small as an atom, as well as bodily perfection and indestructibility.

3.46

Perfection of the body is expressed in beauty of form, vigor, strength, and firm stability.

3.47

Samyama on the real nature of the senses and their process of perception and identification with the separate self leads to mastery over the senses.

3.48

From this one acquires quickness of mind, super-sensual perception and mastery over primordial matter.

3.49

Knowledge of all and sovereignty over all are achieved from a discernment of the difference between sattva and Purusha.

3.50

Vairagya even from this destroys the seed of bondage and leads to Kaivalya (freedom without measure).

3.51
One should not respond with pleasure or pride to the alluring invitations of exalted beings lest harmful attachment recur.

3.52
From samyama on the moment of time and on time sequence, jñana born of viveka, insight born of discernment, is gained.

3.53
Through discernment one realizes the different origins, characteristics, and positions which distinguish two seemingly similar things.

3.54
This jñana born of viveka is liberating, comprehensive, eternal, and freed of time sequence.

3.55
When sattva and Purusha are equal in purity, Kaivalya is there.
It is thus.

Freedom without Measure

4.1
Powers, siddhis may be present at birth, or they may result from drugs, mantras, tapas, or samadhi.

4.2
Transformation into a new state of being is the result of the fullness of the unfolding of the inherent potential of Prakriti.

4.3
The apparent causes of transformation do not in fact bring it about. They merely remove the obstacles to natural growth, as a farmer clears the ground for the crops.

4.4
Fabricating minds arise only from asmita.

4.5

But there is one mind that is the source of the many minds which are involved in activity.

4.6

What is born of dhyana leaves no trace of impressions (samskara).

4.7

The actions of a yogi are beyond good and evil, the actions of others are threefold (good, bad and mixed).

4.8

These actions sow the seeds of vasanas—deep tendencies and habit patterns—which bear fruit corresponding to their nature.

4.9

Because memory and samskaras are both results of the sequence of karma, their continuity is maintained even if their cause is separated from their effect by time, by space or by lifetimes.

4.10

These samskaras are without beginning because the desires that sustain them are everlasting.

4.11

Samskaras are the fruits of previous causes. When the causes are eliminated, there are no further samskaras.

4.12

The past and the future exist within the essential form of the object, but they appear different due to the difference in the paths taken by the properties of that object.

4.13

Manifestations of the properties, whether gross or subtle, are colored by the gunas.

4.14

The "thatness" (*tattvam*) of an object maintains a uniqueness through various transformations of the gunas.

4.15

Although an object remains constant, people's perceptions of it differ because they have different associations.

4.16

The object is not dependent on one mind alone; otherwise, what would become of the object when not cognized by that mind?

4.17

An object is known or unknown depending on whether or not a mind gets colored by it.

4.18

Purusha, owing to its changelessness, is the master of the vrittis of chitta which it always knows.

4.19

Since chitta is an object of perception, it cannot illuminate itself.

4.20

Chitta cannot be aware of its object and of itself at the same time.

4.21

If the perception of one chitta by another chitta were postulated, there would be an endless regression of intelligence and the result would be confusion of memory.

4.22

Chitta becomes self-aware when its consciousness assumes the immovable form of Purusha.

4.23

Chitta which is colored both by the object and the Seer (*Purusha*) is all-apprehending.

4.24

And chitta, despite its countless habits, exists for the sake of the Other (*Purusha*) on whom it is dependent.

4.25

One who sees the distinction between the mind and Atman ceases to cultivate the self.

4.26

Then, deep in viveka, chitta gravitates towards Kaivalya.

4.27

In the process of chitta gravitating to Kaivalya, interruptions may arise due to past samskaras.

4.28

They can be removed in the same manner as the kleshas.

4.29

One who, due to perfect discrimination, is totally non-grasping even of the highest rewards, remains in constant viveka, which is called dharmamegha (cloud of dharma) samadhi.

4.30

From that follows freedom from action colored by kleshas.

4.31

Then all the coverings and impurities of knowledge are totally removed. Because of the vastness of this jñana, little remains to be known.

4.32

Then the sequence of transformations (*parinama*) of the gunas ends, because they have fulfilled their purpose.

4.33

Time succession and its correlates, moments in time, are ended with the ending of parinama.

4.34

The gunas, their purpose fulfilled, return to their original state and pure unbounded Purusha remains forever established in its essential nature. This is Kaivalya, freedom without measure, the Aloneness of the power of seeing. It is thus.

Suggestions for Practical Exploration

All serious students of the *Yoga Sutras* will agree that this remarkable text is a wonderful source of profound psychological and philosophical insights. There is a repeated emphasis in this text on svadhyaya—self-study and self-knowledge. To bring an impartial look at ourselves, with more and more sincerity, it is necessary to gather true self-knowledge. The following exercises may be helpful for this. These exercises can be tried without reference to any specific sutra; but they are correlated with the sutras indicated and may deepen an understanding of these sutras.

Introduction

What is meant by the expression "spiritual search"? What are you searching for?

Have you experienced different levels of attention? How do you distinguish them? What factors affect the level of attention we can bring?

Whatever speaks to us, also reveals us. Write down two or three remarks from any source—from the scriptures, poetry, the sages, or yourself—which you find inspiring and challenging. "God is love" or "All there is is Krishna" are examples.

Yoga Here and Now 1.1

How do you understand being present here and now? Does this have anything to do with time, past, present or future?

In Its True Form 1.3-4

Do you identify yourself with your body or with your mind and feelings, or with the seer who sees through the mind? How would you recognize these different ways of seeing ourselves?

Movements of the Mind 1.5-11

Can you verify the suggestion that the root cause of all distractions is fear or self-importance? Try to see the roots or the causes of distraction in meditation.

Write a minimum of fifty words, but no more than one hundred, on "Who am I?"

Share what you wrote on "Who am I?" with one other person, someone close to you—friend, husband, wife, lover—but only one other person. The condition is that you also listen (or read) her or his piece without approval or disapproval, or judgment or commentary. Ask the other person to try the same while reading your piece.

Stay in Front 1.12-14

How could you verify these two statements: "We do not have steady attention" and "What we attend to is affected by our attention"? Try this by watching your breath, or watch what happens to the attitude of your acquaintances towards you when you listen to them with attention.

Freedom from the Known 1.15-16

Recall your own experience of feeling disillusioned with the world. Is this a disenchantment with the world or with worldliness? Is worldliness in the world or within yourself?

How do you determine whether you have a strong ego or a weak one?

How does the nature of your ego affect learning new things?

A Progressively Settled Mind *1.17-22*

Describe your relationship with your body during different stages of meditation. Is there a stage in which you experience a freedom from the body? If there is, what impulse brings you back to a feeling of "I am the body" rather than "I have a body"?

Surrender to God *1.23-32*

What does God mean to you? Has your image of God changed from childhood to now? Write briefly on your understanding of and your image of God.

What do you most desire? Without considering how it would appear to anyone, how would you express your deepest wish?

Sit in a quiet place with your eyes closed and slowly recite "Om." ("Om" is also written as "Aum" because of the three sounds which make up the vibration. Begin by sounding "A" in the belly, moving up through the chest as "U" is sounded as "oo" and then finish with a nasalization "m" as the vibration moves to the top of the head.) After saying "Om," pay attention to the vibrations which are in the body. Repeat this for a total of four times. How has your state changed?

Tranquil Mind *1.33-39*

You have just heard that a friend has won a great deal of money in a lottery. What is likely to go through your mind? Soon after, you hear that a person who had humiliated you last week in public has suffered severe injuries in a bad car accident. What goes through your mind? What practices do you find helpful in reducing the agitations in your mind and heart?

Listen without judgment to the tone of your own voice as you speak. Does it change in the presence of people you like and those you don't like? Is there a change when speaking to the people who have some authority over you and to those over whom you have some authority? Does your tone betray the fact that you are telling a lie, even an innocent and harmless one, including when you are speaking about things you do not know?

A Clear Mind 1.40-151

Can you recall the conditions which elicited an experience of feeling oneness with respect to your surroundings or with another person? Have you ever had an insight into an idea or a scriptural passage which has not been produced by thought? What conditions allowed such an experience?

Have you encountered situations or experiences where it makes sense to say that we need to prepare ourselves not only to understand truth but also to withstand it?

The Practice of Yoga 2.1-2

What is the nature of spiritual effort? Have you made any?

How do you understand the statement that the major forces running the society are those of reward and punishment? How does this apply to you?

Hindrances 2.3-9

Do you know of occasions in your life when your mind kept returning to some incident in which you felt humiliated or assaulted or victimized in some other fashion? On the other hand, recall the occasions when you were honored and when you felt strong and admired. Which of these two categories has a greater hold on your psyche?

Freedom from Hindrances 2.10-14

How do you understand the effort of pratiprasava (reversal of the flow) in practice?

How can pride of success and sadness about failure be let go?

Yoga for the Ending of Sorrow 2.15-21

How can you verify the Noble Truths of the Buddha which say that the cause of dukkha (suffering) is tanha (selfishness, selfish desire)?

The Seer and the Seen 2.17-21

Look at yourself in a mirror. What do you see? Who sees? Who do you see? Are you the one who sees or are you the one who is seen? Can you look at yourself without thinking, commenting, approving or disapproving?

Freedom from Ignorance 2.22-27

Do you feel there is a reason or a purpose for your existence? How is this purpose served by your incarnation in this body at this time and this place?

Self-Restraint 2.28-31

Look at yourself in relationship with one other person to see if you are free of himsa (manipulation, violation, imposition) or not.

Observances 2.32-34

Try for a day not to express any negative thoughts or feelings. Choose one feeling such as anger, jealousy, or impatience which occasionally takes hold of you. What would be required for you not to be assaulted by this feeling?

Being Established in Yama and Niyama 2.35-45

How would you answer in your own case, regarding money, information and position in the society, "What is enough?", or "How much is enough?", "When is it enough?", "Enough for what?"

Right Alignment 2.46-48

How does your mental posture and emotional state affect your physical posture? And vice versa?

If you have seen directly or in a photograph the famous sculpture by Rodin called "The Thinker," would you say that the thinker in the sculpture is sitting in a good posture for clear thinking?

The Breath of Life 2.49-53

After you spend some time simply breathing in and breathing out and paying attention to the breath, how would you respond to the question "Do I breathe or am I breathed?"

Withdrawal of the Senses 2.54-55

Have you had experiences in which certain kinds of sounds enhanced silence? Also, have you encountered situations in which external silence has produced an emotional agitation? What tentative conclusions can you draw from these experiences about the relationship between external sound and a feeling of silence?

Total Attention 3.1-8

Look at a flower or a plant for some time. Can you watch and say what the causes of the fluctuation of our attention are and what stands in the way of samyama?

Transformations of the Mind 3.9-15

Watching your own mind in a quiet place, can you say whether the noise in the mind is the basic ground with occasional moments of silence; or is silence the ground with occasional movements in the mind? Has this balance changed since you started your practice of yoga?

Subtle Knowledge 3.16-34

What are your major powers or talents (such as intelligence, charm, interpersonal skill, or any other)? What do they serve?

Siddhis as Impediments 3.35-37

You have just heard that a friend of yours has developed extraordinary powers. What is your reaction to this news?

Mastery over Natural Forces 3.38-49

Do you wish to have siddhis (super-powers)? Should you? What will you do with them?

Unconditioned Freedom *3.50-55*

How do you distinguish between "freedom for myself" and "freedom from myself"? What practical implications does this distinction have in life?

Subtle Impressions *4.1-11*

Can you identify in yourself two natures—lower and higher, or carnal and spiritual? What are the tendencies and habits of these two natures?

Objective Reality *4.12-17*

What do you think is the relationship between the existence of something and its perception by someone?

Mind and Spirit *4.18-26*

The basic question asked by Patañjali is, "What is the right relationship between Prakriti and Purusha?" How would you phrase this question for yourself, and then what will be the direction of your response?

Freedom Without Measure *4.27-34*

There is a story of three old monks in a Jewish monastery, who waited for the Messiah (an avatar) to come. After many years, they found themselves irritated with each other and complaining about the conditions. Finally they traveled to a distant monastery and spoke to the abbot there. The abbot told them that the Messiah had already come, and that he was one of them. They now looked at each other a little differently.

If you have been assured that one of your friends, or you yourself, is the Messiah or avatar or a jivan mukta (liberated while still alive), what will change in your relationships?

May We All Be Blessed Into Usefulness

Write down three insights from the *Yoga Sutras*, which you wish to carry with you in your life. Arrange them in order of significance to your own search.

ACKNOWLEDGEMENTS

First and foremost I would like to thank my friend and editor, Priscilla Murray. Without her help, this book could not have been written.

I am grateful to the Theosophical Society for providing a venue and a context to teach a course on Patañjali's *Yoga Sutras* in the School of the Wisdom in Adyar, Chennai, India, and again in the Krotona School of Theosophy in Ojai, California. Many students in these courses undertook the exercises which are included in the book and helped in checking their suitability and usefulness.

I am very grateful to my friend and fellow searcher Dennis Pence for his generosity of the spirit and of the heart.

There are two sages who have been sources of great inspiration and clarity for me. They are Madame Jeanne de Salzmann and J. Krishnamurti. Their teachings have been constant reminders of the existence of higher levels of being and the possibility of connecting with these. Whenever I was unclear about the meaning of any sutra in Patañjali's *Yoga Sutras*, I would turn to their teachings and find helpful insights. No words are adequate to express my gratitude to them; I feel blessed having had some contact with them.

Glossary of Selected Sanskrit and Pali Words

This glossary provides a quick reference for useful Sanskrit and Pali words. It is hoped that readers will become familiar with the Sanskrit words for the central concepts which cannot be translated adequately with a single word in English.

In the glossary, the English phonetic spelling of the words is followed by the word spelled with diacritical marks, using the ususal scholarly conventions, which provides a more precise pronunciation guide.

abhinivesha (abhiniveśa): momentum to continue in the state one is in

abhyasa (abhyāsa): practice, repetition

adhyatma (adhyātma): the deepest self

ahamkara (ahaṃkāra): egotism, sense of self, pride; literally, "I am the doer"

ahimsa (ahiṃsā): nonviolation, nonviolence

akinchan (akiñchan): self-naughting, freedom from egotism

alinga (aliṅga): traceless, without a mark, the meeting ground of manifestation and non-manifestation

ananda (ānanda): delight, bliss, joy

antaraya (antarāya): interference

aparigraha (aparigrahā): non-possession, non-grasping, non-covetousness

asana (āsana): posture, alignment; one of the five external limbs of yoga according to Patañjali

asmita (asmitā): egoism, "I am this"

asteya: non-stealing

ashtanga (aṣṭāṅga): eight-limbed

Atman (ātman): Self, Spirit, soul, the deepest part of a person; often used in the nominative form ***atma***

Aum: same as Om

avatara (avatāra): descent of a deity; incarnation—particularly of *Viṣṇu*, the maintainer of cosmic order

avidya (avidyā, avijjā in Pali): ignorance, illusion, sometimes personified as Maya

Bhagavad Gita (Bhagavad-gītā, Bhagavad Gītā): Song of the Blessed One; perhaps the single most important work to originate from India. It is a part of the great epic Mahabharata; date range 600–200 BCE.

bhakti: devotion, adoration, love and worship

bhakti yoga: the way of love

bodhi: perfect knowledge or wisdom (by which a person becomes buddha)

Brahma (Brahmā): first of the triad of personalized gods, ***Brahma-Vishnu-Shiva***; the Universal Spirit manifested as Creator; the Great Being

brahmacharya: dwelling in Brahman; the student stage of life; containment; sexual continence

Brahman: Godhead, Deitas, Absolute, self-existent nonpersonal Spirit, the Ultimate Reality; literally, Vastness

brahmanda (brahmāṇḍa): cosmos; literally, egg of Brahman

brahmin (brāhmaṇa): one who has sacred knowledge; one belonging to the first of the four castes

Buddha: awakened, awake, enlightened, liberated; used as a proper name of the historical Siddhartha Gautama

buddhi: soul, will, intellect, integrated intelligence, understanding

chakra: center of energy related to the human organism

chitta: mind, consciousness, psyche

darshana (darśana): point of view, perspective, school of philosophy

Dhammapada: an early Buddhist document discussing the chief values of life and the path which leads to enlightenment

dharma: law, order, responsibility for the maintenance of order, duty, religion, righteousness, obligation, teaching

dharana (dhāraṇā): concentration, focused attention, one of the three internal limbs of Patañjali Yoga

dhyana (dhyāna): meditation, contemplation; one of the three internal limbs of Yoga. Dhyana becomes Ch'an in Chinese, Ŝon in Korean, and Zen in Japanese

dhyana yoga (dhyāna yoga): the way of contemplation

dukkha (the Sanskrit equivalent of this Pali word is ***duḥkha)***: suffering, anguish, affliction, angst, sorrow, frustration

dvesha (dveṣa): aversion, dislike, hate

ekagrata parinama (***ekāgratā pariṇāma***): transformation in the state of one-pointedness

gopi: (literally, cowgirl) In the loveplay of Krishna and the gopis, the gopis represent the human soul

guna (guṇa): fundamental quality of nature, strand, constituent; the three gunas—sattva, rajas, tamas—are the three fundamental constituents of the whole of Prakṛti (Nature) even at the most subtle level

hatha yoga (***haṭha yoga***): physical yoga with an emphasis on asanas and pranayama

himsa (hiṃsā): violence, violation, manipulation, the opposite of ahimsa.

ishta devata (iṣhṭa devatā): one's chosen deity

Ishvara (Īśvara): God, the supreme Being, personal Deity

jagrata(jāgrata) : the ordinary state of waking consciousness

jñana (jñāna): gnosis, wisdom, sacred knowledge (as distinct from vijnana which is profane knowledge, science)

jñana yoga (jñana yoga): the way of knowledge

kaivalya: freedom without measure, the highest state of consciousness, Aloneness

kala (kāla): time; also identified with Yama (Lord of death as well as of dharma); the root word is *kal*, which means to calculate or enumerate

kama (kāma): wish, desire, longing; Kama is god of love and desire

karma: act, action, work; result, effect; law of karma (cause and effect) is cosmic, that applies to moral and psychological, as well as physical, spheres

karma yoga: the way of sacred action

klesha (kleśa): obstacle, impediment

Krishna (Kṛṣṇa): the divine teacher in the Bhagavad Gita; the eighth incarnation (avatar) of Vishnu; linguistically, "Krishna" is derived from two roots, meaning "the dark one" and "the attractor"

kriya (kriyā): practice, action; Kriya Yoga consists of tapas, svadhyaya, ishvara-pranidhana

kshatriya (kṣatriya): the warrior or administrator caste

kshudra brahmanda (*kṣudra brahmāṇda*): microcosmos; literally, small egg of Brahman

linga (liṅga): mark, sign, trace; Shiva-linga is the phallus of Shiva; linga sharira is the subtle body which does not die at the death of the physical body

manas: lower mind, reason; the faculty by which objects of sense affect buddhi

maya (māyā): illusion, unreality, deception, power; from the same root as "measure"; Maya is illusion personified, identified with Prakriti

moksha (mokṣa): unconditioned and uncaused freedom, liberation

mukti: freedom, liberation, final beatitude; same as moksha

nidra (nidrā): in the Upanishads it is a level of consciousness higher than the level of svapna; literally, sleep

nirbija samadhi (nirbīja samādhi): seedless samadhi

nirvana (nirvāṇa, nibbāna in Pali): extinction of tanha (selfish craving), the highest felicity

nirvitarka: super-rational, beyond thought

nishkama karma (niśkāma karma): action without selfish desire

nishkarma kama (niśkarma kāma): desire without action, fantasy

nivritti (nivṛtti): returning to the source, withdrawal, tendency opposite to pravritti

niyama: restraint, control; one of the five outer limbs of Yoga

Om: primordial vibration, most sacred syllable; same as Aum

pāda (pada): section, path; literally, foot

parinama (pariṇāma): transformation

prajña (prajñā): insight, wisdom, understanding

prakrita (prākṛta): natural, unrefined, vulgar, common

prakriti (prakṛti): nature; materiality; sometimes same as maya

prana (prāṇa): subtle energy, breath; equivalent to Chi (Qi) in Chinese thought

pranayama (prāṇāyāma): regulation of prana, breath control; one of the five outer limbs of Yoga

pranidhana (pranidhāṇa): dedication, respect, surrender

pratiprasava: reverse flow

pratyak chetana (pratyak chetanā): inwardness; to turn one's thoughts inward

pratyahara (pratyāhāra): drawing back the senses; one of the five outer limbs of Yoga

pravritti (pravṛtti): manifestation, outward and expansive tendency, as opposed to nivritti

Purusha (Puruṣa): Transcendent Person, Supreme Being, also identified with *Atman* and *Brahman*

raga (rāga): liking, attraction, melody; opposite of dvesha

rajas: the guna of passion and activity

raja yoga (rāja yoga): the royal yoga, another name for the yoga taught in the *Yoga Sutras*, also associated with dhyana yoga and Patanjali's yoga

Rig Veda (Ṛg Veda): the oldest of the four Vedas and the oldest text in any Indo-European language; the oldest parts may date back to 3000 BCE

rita (ṛta): cosmic order

ritambhara (ṛtambharā): full of order, truth-bearing

sabija samadhi (sabīja samādhi): samadhi with seed

sadhaka (sādhaka): aspirant, practitioner

sadhana (sādhanā): practice, effort, quest

sakshatkara (sākśātkāra): direct perception

samadhi (samādhi): timeless insight, free attention, integration, synthesis, tranquility, profound meditation; the eighth and last limb of Yoga

samapatti (samāpatti): fusion, union, coincidence, coming together

samsara (saṃsāra): world, secular life, worldly illusion; the circuit of mundane existence; the cosmic flux

samskara (saṃskāra): impression, influence

samyama (saṃyama): total attention, perfect discipline; a combination of dhyana, dharana and samadhi in Patañjali' s yoga.

samkalpa (saṃkalpa): imagination, self-will, or desire-will

Sankhya (Sāṇkhya): one of the important schools of philosophy in India, often closely associated with Yoga

sanyasi (sanyāsi): One who has renounced

Sanskrit (Saṃskṛta): name of the sacred language of India

sanskrita (saṃskṛta): well-formed, perfected, refined, educated

sattva: the guṇa of lucidity and mindfulness

satya: truth

savitarka: with thought, rational

shakti (śakti): energy, power, the feminine counterpart of Shiva

Shankara (Śaṇkara): one of the greatest philosophers of India who propounded Advaita (nondual) Vedanta

sharira (śarīra): body (including the mind and emotions)

shastra (śāstra): teaching, sacred book

shraddha (śraddhā): faith, trust

Shiva (Śiva): auspicious; lord of sleep; third of the Hindu triad of personalized gods, Brahma-Vishnu-Shiva; lord of transformation; awakener

shruti (śruti): that which has been heard, revelation

shudra (śūdra): worker, laborer, one of the four castes

shunyata (śūnyatā): zeroness, emptiness, the doctrine that anything in isolation from the whole is insignificant and nonexistent

siddhi: power, accomplishment

smriti (smṛti): mindfulness, memory, remembered tradition

sushupta (suṣupta): a state of consciousness in nidra

sutra (sūtra): aphorism; litterally, thread

svabhava (svabhāva): inner calling, essential nature, own being

svadharma: dharma (obligation) corresponding to one's svabhava

svadhyaya (svādhyāya): self-study, study of sacred texts

svakarma: karma (action) corresponding to one's svabhava

svapna: in the Upanishads, it is a level of consciousness higher than of jagrata; literally, dream

tamas: the guna corresponding to inertia and sloth, as well as stability

tanha (tanhā in Pali, tṛṣṇā iṇ Sanskrit): selfishness, egotistic craving, desire

tapas: heat; spiritual austerity, penance, effort, self-discipline

tapasya (tapasyā): effort, sustained practice, austerity

tattva: the essential nature, suchness, thatness

turiya (turīya): the highest state of consciousness in the Upanishads; literally, the fourth

Upanishad (Upaniṣad): important sacred writings of the Hindus, usually philosophical in nature. These constitute the concluding portion of the Vedas, and number over 200 different works, dating between 800 and 500 BCE.

upeksha (upekṣa): impartiality, equanimity

vairagya (vairāgya): non-identificaiton, detachment, withdrawal from the world of reward and punishment

vaishya (vaiśya): the merchant caste

vasana (vāsanā): habit, pattern, innate and deep tendency

vishayavati (viśayavati): sensation; literally, object-centered

Veda: the most sacred literature of the Hindus; knowledge. There are four Vedas, the oldest being the Rig Veda, composed around 1500 BCE or before.

Vedanta (Vedānta): the name of the most influential school of philosophy in India; literally, the end of knowledge

vibhuti (vibhūti): splendor, glory, power

vichara (vichāra): thought, reflection, reason

vidya (vidyā): knowledge, wisdom

vishesha (viśeṣa): special, particular, unique

virya (vīrya): energy, vitality

Vishnu (Viṣṇu): second of the Hindu triad of gods, Brahma-Vishnu-Shiva; the preserver and the sustainer

vitarka: reasoning

viveka: discernment, discrimination

vritti (vṛtti): movement of the mind, distraction, modification, fluctuation

yajña (yajña): sacrifice; a sacrificial rite or ceremony; an exchange between levels

yama: one of the five outer limbs of yoga

Yama: Lord of death as well as of ḍharma;

yoga: integration, union, the art of yoking, joining, attaching; any path with the aim of union with Ishvara or the Supreme Spirit

Yoga Sutra (Yoga Sūtra): the most important text of yoga, attributed to the great sage Patañjali

BIBLIOGRAPHY

Anirvan, Sri. *Inner Yoga: Selected Writings of Sri Anirvan*. Sandpoint: Morning Light Press, 2007.

Aurobindo, Sri. trans. *The Upanishads*. Twin Lakes: Lotus Press, 1996.

———. *The Message of the Gita*. Pondicherry, India: Sri Aurobindo Ashram Press, 1984.

Badrinath, Chaturvedi. *Swami Vivekananda: The Living Vedanta*. New Delhi: Penguin Books India, 2006.

Blake, William. *The Complete Poetry and Prose of William Blake*. New York: Bantam Doubleday Dell, 1988.

Case, Margaret, ed. *The Inner Journey: Views from the Hindu Tradition*. Sandpoint: Morning Light Press, 2007.

Chakravarty, Amiya, ed. *A Tagore Reade*r. Beacon Press: Boston, 1966.

Chapple, Christopher and Yogi Anand Viraj. *The Yoga Sutras of Patañjali: An Analysis of the Sanskrit with Accompanying English Translation*. Delhi: Sri Satguru Publications, 1990.

Daumal, René. *Mount Analogue*. trans. Roger Shattuck. Boston: Shambhala

Publications, 1992.

Desikachar, T. K. V. *The Heart of Yoga*. Rochester: Inner Traditions, 1999.

Eliot, Thomas Sterns. *Four Quartets*, London: Faber and Faber, 1996.

Feuerstein, Georg. *The Yoga-Sutra of Patañjali: A New Translation and Commentary*. Rochester, VT: Inner Traditions, 1989.

Gurdjieff, G. I. *Beelzebub's Tales to His Grandson*. New York: Harcourt, Brace & Company, 1950. London: Routledge & Kegan Paul, 1950. and E. P. Dutton & Co., Inc., 1964.

Hartranft, Chip. *The Yoga-Sutra of Patañjali: A New Translation with Commentary*. Boston: Shambhala, 2003.

Johnston, William, ed. *The Cloud of Unknowing and The Book of Privy Counseling*. New York: Image Doubleday, 1996.

Krishnamurti, J. *Krishnamurti's Journals*. San Fransciso: Harper & Row, 1982.

———. *Krishnamurti's Notebook*. Ojai: Krishnamurti Publications of America, 2002.

Miller, Barbara Stoler, trans. *Yoga: Discipline of Freedom; The Yoga Sutra Attributed to Patañjali*. New York: Bantam, 1998.

———. *The Bhagavad Gita: Krishna's Counsel in War*. New York: Bantam, 1986.

Needleman, Jacob, ed. *The Inner Journey: Views from the Gurdjieff Work*. Sandpoint: Morning Light Press, 2008.

Novak, Philip, ed. *The Inner Journey: Views from the Buddhist Tradition*. Sandpoint: Morning Light Press, 2005.

Ouspensky, P. D. *In Search of the Miraculous: Fragments of an Unknown Teaching*. Orlando: Harcourt, 2001.

Radhakrishnan, S., ed. and trans. *The Principal Upanishads*. London: Allen & Unwin, 1966.

Ravindra, Ravi. *The Spiritual Roots of Yoga: Royal Path to Freedom*. Sandpoint: Morning Light Press, 2006.

———. *Heart Without Measure: Gurdjieff Work with Madame de Salzmann*. Sandpoint: Morning Light Press, 2004.

———. *The Gospel of John in the Light of Indian Mysticism*. Rochester: Inner Traditions. 2004. Earlier published as *The Yoga of the Christ* and as *Christ the Yogi*.

———. *Pilgrim Without Boundaries*. Sandpoint: Morning Light Press, 2003.

———. *Centered Self without Being Self-Centered: Remembering Krishnamurti*. Sandpoint: Morning Light Press, 2003.

———. *Science and the Sacred*. Wheaton: Quest Books, 2002.

———. *J. Krishnamurti: Two Birds on One Tree*. Wheaton: Quest Books, 1995.

Reymond, Lizelle and Sri Anirvan. *To Live Within*. Sandpoint: Morning Light Press, 2007.

Rilke, Rainer Maria. *Letters to a Young Poet*. trans. M. D. Herter Norton. New York: Norton, 1993.

About the Author

Ravi Ravindra received his early education in India before moving to Canada. He has been a Member of the Institute of Advanced Study in Princeton, and a Fellow of the Indian Institute of Advanced Study in Shimla. At present Dr. Ravindra is Professor Emeritus at Dalhousie University, Halifax, Canada, where he was Professor and Chair of Comparative Religion and Adjunct Professor of Physics.

In addition to a profound study of the great traditions, Ravi Ravindra has had a longstanding and serious engagement with spiritual search. He has been nourished by his close association with Krishnamurti, with Zen and with the Gurdjieff Work. He has been practicing yoga for more than half a century. He received blessings and instruction from the great yoga exponent Sri Krishnamacharya and studied with Sri TKV Desikachar at the Krishnamacharya Yoga Mandiram in Chennai, India.

Other books by Ravi Ravindra include:

Heart Without Measure: Gurdjieff Work with Madame de Salzmann
Krishnamurti: Two Birds on One Tree
The Gospel of John in the Light of Indian Mysticism
Science and the Sacred: Eternal Wisdom in a Changing World
Centered Self without Being Self-Centered: Remembering Krishnamurti
Pilgrim Without Boundaries
The Spiritual Roots of Yoga: Royal Path to Freedom